McGRAW HILL EDUCATION WINNING EDGE WE SERIES

Challenges *to*
INTERNAL SECURITY OF INDIA

GS PAPER III

For Civil Services Main Examination

About the Authors

Ashok Kumar did his B.Tech and M. Tech from Indian Institute of Technology (IIT) Delhi. He joined the Indian Police Service (IPS) in 1989 and has served in various challenging assignments in UP and Uttarakhand. He joined the Central Reserve Police Force (CRPF) on deputation in 2009 and is presently IG (Punjab Frontier), Border Security Force (BSF). He received the UN Medal for serving in strife-torn Kosovo in 2001. He was awarded the Indian Police Medal for meritorious Service in 2006 and President's Police Medal for Distinguished Services in 2013. He has authored a path-breaking book titled 'Human in Khaki', 'खाकी में इंसान' which received GB Pant Award from Bureau of Police Research & Development (BPR&D), MHA.

Email: ashokips89@gmail.com
website: www.humaninkhaki.com

Vipul is B.Tech. from Malaviya National Institute of Technology (MNIT), Jaipur. He was a student of Tata Institute of Social Sciences (TISS), Mumbai.

He has been selected in UPSC Civil Services Examination 2011 and has joined The Delhi and Andaman & Nicobar Islands Police Service(DANIPS).

McGRAW HILL EDUCATION WINNING WE EDGE SERIES

Challenges *to* INTERNAL SECURITY OF INDIA

GS PAPER III

For Civil Services Main Examination

Ashok Kumar, IPS

IG, BSF

Vipul

DANIPS

McGraw Hill Education (India) Private Limited

NEW DELHI

McGraw Hill Education Offices

New Delhi New York St Louis San Francisco Auckland Bogotá Caracas Kuala Lumpur Lisbon London Madrid Mexico City Milan Montreal San Juan Santiago Singapore Sydney Tokyo Toronto

McGraw Hill Education (India) Private Limited

Published by McGraw Hill Education (India) Private Limited
P-24, Green Park Extension, New Delhi 110 016

Challenges to Internal Security of India

Fifth reprint 2015
RQDACRCVRXRDA

Print Edition
ISBN(13): 978-93-392-0419-8
ISBN(10): 93-392-0419-0

E-book Edition
ISBN(13): 978-93-392-1327-5
ISBN(10): 93-392-1327-0

Managing Director: *Kaushik Bellani*

Deputy General Manager—Test Prep and School: *Tanmoy Roychowdhury*
Publishing Manager—Test Prep: *K N Prakash*
Assistant Sponsoring Editor—*Bhavna Malhotra*
Asst Manager (Developmental Editing): *Anubha Srivastava*
Asst Manager—Production: *Medha Arora*
Product Specialist: *Vikas Sharma*

General Manager—Production: *Rajender P Ghansela*
Manager—Production: *Reji Kumar*

Typeset at The Composers, 260, C.A. Apt., Paschim Vihar, New Delhi 110 063, and printed at Avon Printers, Jawahar Nagar, Ind. Area, Shahdara, Delhi 110 094.

Cover Printer: SDR Printers
Visit us at: www.mheducation.co.in

Disclaimer

The views and opinions expressed in this book are purely that of the Author and not of any Government body or agency or the Border Security Force (BSF) or the Publisher. The book is published with the intention to only provide information related to the topics given in the syllabus of the Civil Services Main Examination.

References / Acknowledgements

1. Report of 2nd Administrative Reforms Commission (ARC)
2. Annual Reports of Ministry of Home Affairs (MHA)
3. MHA Website
4. Websites of various Security Forces likes BSF, CRPF, CISF, etc.
5. Wikipedia
6. BSF publication—'The Man Who Saw Tomorrow'

Preface

The idea of this book came to my mind when some aspirants appearing for the Civil Services examination approached me for guidance regarding the topics on Internal Security and Disaster Management in the new syllabus framed by the UPSC for the main examination.

When I saw the syllabus, I realised that it may be quite cumbersome for someone who has not dealt with the topic at all. The syllabus has been so framed that it would not be easy for candidates to answer the questions related to the topic unless they have a reasonable depth of understanding of the subject. The syllabus covers not only the important aspects of the emerging challenges of internal security that India faces today, but its language was also highly technical. One could easily be misled about the areas that needed to be studied to cover the whole of the syllabus. One needs to have a deep understanding of the complex issues of national security to get a grip on the syllabus.

When I discussed with these young aspirants about the syllabus and what they had been studying, I was surprised about the perception they had about the new syllabus. I found that the syllabus had not been interpreted in the proper perspective by the aspirants and many a times the focus was diverted from the real issues. This motivated me to write this book to help the young aspirants, so that they would not be misguided by the various coaching institutes and also would not have to spend hours surfing the internet, finding out the real meaning of 'External State and Non-State Actors' or 'Linkages between Development and Spread of Extremism'.

Internal Security is a vast subject. India faces tremendous challenges on its internal security front. Kashmir and North-East have been long-standing problem areas, but more recently, the ugly face of terrorism has been raising its head all across the hinterland of the country. The problem has been aggravated by transnational organized criminals joining hands with various anti-India forces. Naxalism is now spread over 223 districts of the country which comprises almost one third of the whole country's area and population.

Apart from terrorism / extremism, we are also facing law and order issues due to various kinds of conflicts caused by communal, caste and ethnic tensions as well as regional aspirations. The new age technology like internet, mobile, social media has brought new challenges including the cyber security. The new age technology also makes it easier for the spread of various ideologies and hate campaigns.

The Uttarakhand disaster of June 2013, that resulted in over 5000 deaths has demonstrated how poorly we are equipped in managing natural disasters of gigantic magnitude. Therefore, we have included a chapter on Disaster Management at the end.

We have incorporated many invaluable recommendations made by the Administrative Reforms Commission (2nd ARC) so that candidates need not go through the whole ARC Reports for preparation of topics related to internal security. Apart from the ARC reports, we have also included suggestions from important Government Committees and Reports of MHA wherever necessary on matters related to internal security.

I am sure that this book will give the young aspirants a fair idea of the security challenges that our country faces today. Our approach has been to explain the historical background, current status and the way forward to deal with these challenges. My efforts are to make this book most authentic on the subject to make it a valuable tool for aspirants preparing for the prestigious civil service examination in the country. This book is meant to provide a conceptual framework to understand and analyse the issues involved. However, internal security being a rapidly changing subject, aspirants are advised to focus on current issues related to internal security and keep themselves updated.

My co-author Vipul has been associated with me all through this process. We have been discussing on what all should be included in a particular chapter and what key issues should be made part of this book. He has been a great help throughout.

I would like to thank Mr. Amit Kumar Jain for his significant contribution in shaping the book. His suggestions have been very useful specially in the chapter on Left Wing Extremism. My thanks to Mr. O.P. Upadhyaya, Commandant BSF, for his contribution in chapters on "Border Management" and "Security Forces and Agencies". My special thanks to Mr. Nikhilesh Neogi who has sacrificed his weekends to help me in compiling and editing the book. I am also thankful to Mr. Arun Bhadula for his valuable contribution. My special thanks also to Mr. Prakash Kannath of McGraw Hill Education for his continuous and fruitful engagement during the publishing of the book.

I am sure that this book will not only help the UPSC aspirants in GS paper III of the main examination but also for the Essay paper as it will give a clear insight into the issues so that candidates can plan and organize their essays related to such topics in a much better way. The key issues discussed in this book will also be of help to candidates lucky enough to face the interview board for their Personality Test.

I wish all readers the best in their endeavour. Suggestions for further improvement are welcome and can be sent to ashokips89@gmail.com

Ashok Kumar

Contents

CHAPTER 1

Internal Security

1.1 Internal and External Security

At the outset, we shall briefly differentiate between internal and external security of a country before we discuss the various aspects of internal security.

Internal security is the security of a country within its borders. This basically implies maintenance of peace and law and order, and upholding sovereignty of the country within its territory.

Internal security is different from external security to the extent that *external security* is security against aggression by a foreign country. External security is solely the responsibility of the armed forces of the country, while internal security comes under the purview of the police, which can be supported by the armed police forces, if required.

In India, the **Ministry of Home Affairs** (MHA) takes care of internal security, while external security comes under the **Ministry of Defence**. In many countries, MHA is also called the Ministry of Internal Affairs or Ministry of Homeland Security.

1.1.1 Classification of Threat

Kautilya wrote in *Arthashastra* that a state can be at risk from four kinds of threats:

- Internal
- External

- Internally aided external
- Externally aided internal

India's internal security threat perceptions are a mix of all four shades of threats defined above.

The changing external environment also impacts our internal security. Events in Sri Lanka, Pakistan, Bangladesh, Nepal and Myanmar have direct or indirect linkages with our internal security. Therefore, it can be said that in today's information and digital age, security threats, both internal and external, are inter-related and cannot be seen in isolation from each other.

Over the years, the challenges to our internal security have grown manifold and assumed alarming proportions. Internal security problems have started affecting our country's growth and development. This is now one of the prime concerns in the top echelons of the Government.

Therefore, it is no surprise that the UPSC has included internal security as a separate topic in the Civil Services Main Examination since 2013.

➤ 1.1.2 Attributes of Internal Security

The main attributes of internal security are:

- Secure territorial integrity and protect internal sovereignty
- Maintain domestic peace
- Prevalence of law and order
- Rule of law and equality before law—law of the land should protect everyone irrespective of status
- Absence of fear from the feared implying individual freedom for people as guaranteed by the Constitution
- Peaceful co-existence and communal harmony

➤ 1.2 Major Challenges to Internal Security

Independence for India came with some inherited problems related to internal security. The issue of the accession of the state of Jammu and Kashmir to India also came with its own set of problems related to our internal security. The division of the pre-independence India into two nations resulted in large scale unforeseen violence that claimed millions of lives. Thus was born the menace of communalism which was visible again and again in various riots thereafter.

As an emerging nation, we hoped to overcome these problems and embark upon a path of national reconstruction and consolidation, but progress has been hampered by various challenges to internal security faced by the country.

Over the years, India's internal security problems have multiplied due to linguistic riots, inter-state disputes, caste and ethnic tensions, etc. In 1956, the country was forced to redefine its inter-state boundaries due to linguistic riots.

Major Challenges

1. Hinterland terrorism — International and domestic
2. J&K militancy & terrorism
3. Insurgency in North- east
4. Left-wing extremism
5. Organised crime and its nexus with terrorism
6. Communalism
7. Caste and ethnic tensions
8. Regionalism and inter-state disputes
9. Cyber-crime and cyber-security
10. Border management
11. Coastal security

The 1950s also saw the North-east going up in flames, when in 1954 Phizo raised the banner of revolt in Nagaland and the fire spread to Mizoram, Manipur and Tripura.

The later part of the sixties saw the rise of Naxalism. At the time of independence, India was an under-developed country and had taken up the task of rebuilding the country. The country adopted the equitable and inclusive growth model for growth and development. But, over the years, it has become evident that we have failed on many counts and poverty, unemployment and under-development prevail in the interior regions of the country. This situation was exploited by various people to pose a very dangerous challenge to the country's internal security in the form of Maoism / Naxalism / Left-Wing Extremism. In 2006, the then Prime Minister even admitted that this was perhaps the biggest challenge to the country's internal security.

The eighties witnessed the growth of the terrorist movement in Punjab, aided and abetted by a hostile neighbour. The nineties saw the beginning of militancy in Kashmir which has slowly become a pan-India phenomena with the onslaught of international terrorism in the hinterland during the past decade. The rise of Indian Mujahideen (IM) has been another dangerous phenomena in the last decade. This has again been supported by the unfriendly neighbour as became clearly evident during the 26/11 terror attack in Mumbai. As a result, the Centre initiated a number of concrete measures to strengthen its anti-terrorism apparatus.

Transnational organised criminals/mafias have given further boost to international terrorism by forging linkages between organised crime and terrorism. Their funding and modus operandi has mainly been arms smuggling, drugs trafficking, hawala transactions, money laundering and pumping of fake Indian currency notes (FICN) to different parts of the country.

Cyber security is the latest challenge. We could be the target of a cyber-war which could jeopardise our security as most of our vital installations are now based on cyber systems. Any failure to check cyber attacks could be fatal to our economy and security. The Snowden revelations (Wikileaks) of 2013 have exposed the extent of espionage that is possible through cyber networks. The phenomenal growth of the internet and mobile communication has demonstrated that social media could play a vital role in spreading disinformation and fanning violence. The exodus of Northeast students from the southern states in 2012 and the Muzaffarnagar riots in 2013 are some examples of the problems being created due to the fast growing communication systems.

Border management is important for containing threats to our internal security. A weak border management can result in infiltration of terrorists and illegal immigrants from various borders and smuggling of contraband items like arms, drugs and counterfeit currency. There has been an increase in hostility against illegal migrants in the North-east. We are yet to find a satisfactory solution, be it political, social or economical, to this problem.

There are also some non-traditional, non-military threats to our security. These include climatic security, diseases and epidemics, energy and water, food issues, resource wars, poverty and economic disparity, etc. These have not been included in the scope of the book.

1.3 Factors Responsible for Internal Security Problems

There are various reasons, both historical and non-historical, which cause problems for our internal security. These have been discussed in detail in the forthcoming chapters. However, a few root causes are mentioned below:

- Unfriendly neighbours
- Poverty
- Unemployment
- Inequitable growth
- Widening gap between haves and have nots
- Failure on administrative front or Governance deficit
- Increasing communal divide
- Increasing caste awareness and caste tensions
- Rise of contentious politics based on sectarian, ethnic, linguistic or other divisive criteria
- Porous borders having very tough terrain
- Poor criminal justice system and large scale corruption leading to nexus between criminals, police and politicians with the result that organised crime goes on unabated.

We inherited the first three factors at the time of independence. We have failed to resolve all the three issues. Unfortunately, we have added more factors which have multiplied our internal security problems. The fourth, fifth and sixth factors in the above list can be termed as administrative failures and the seventh, eighth and ninth could be due to the rise of partisan politics. The last two can be attributed to a pronounced deficit of governance. Every problem gets highlighted because of these factors and hostile neighbours leave no opportunity to exploit internal conditions for the pursuit of their own agenda. The declared policy of Pakistan's ISI 'to bleed India through a thousand cuts' proves the points.

1.4 Internal Security Doctrine

1.4.1. Internal Security Doctrine should include the following key elements

- Political
- Socio-economic
- Governance
- Police & Security Forces
- Centre–State Coordination
- Intelligence
- Border Management
- Cyber Security

1. Political First, we need to know the nature of the challenge to our internal security. It could be secessionist, separatist or even regional in nature. We have to analyse the causative factors of various types of movements and see whether the demands are within the constitutional framework or not. As a matter of principle, we have to deal the secessionist movements with a heavy hand. Separatist elements have to be kept at a distance. We need a clear policy with stringent laws to deal with such elements. On the other hand, regional aspirations and ethnic demands require reasonably softer and sympathetic approach.
2. Socio-economic Socio-economic factors are also at the back of many movements which are big threats to the internal security of the country. Many a times, there are genuine socio-economic grievances of a section of the society arising from acute poverty, unemployment and displacement. In such cases, our approach has to be different. We need to analyse the factors causing the socio-economic grievances and address all the connected issues. Equitable growth and development is the spirit of our Constitution. Therefore, we have to ensure that development reaches all sections of the society and there are no regional disparities.

3. Governance Lack of good governance also provides a tool in the hands of anti-establishment elements, who pose a challenge to the internal security of the country. Such elements take advantage of mismanagement and corruption in government schemes, poor implementation of laws and absence of government machinery in the remote areas. Governance on all fronts becomes an issue whether it is civil administration or policing of the area or the whole of criminal justice system. It is the duty of the state to control all the malaise in governance and provide good governance to the remotest of the areas and control corruption. Otherwise, development of remote areas will be nearly impossible.

4. Police & Security Forces It has been seen that, at times allegations of police atrocities and police indifference towards people's problems, aggravate internal security problems. We have seen many times that agitations are directed against the police or the security forces. Demand for removal of AFSPA is one such example. Police needs to be sensitized so that it becomes people friendly. We need to carry out police reforms so that the police is seen as a neutral, transparent and professional body. Other security forces aiding state police

also need to increase their understanding of the local situation and maintain highest order of efficiency. They need to coordinate with the state police and help achieve overall goal of maintaining the internal security.

5. Centre–State Coordination Lack of centre–state coordination also leads to many problems related to internal security. This coordination problem exists in all areas from intelligence to operations. We need to develop an institutional framework which resolves all these centre-state coordination problems and ensures synergy at all levels.

6. Intelligence Intelligence is a major component of Internal Security. We need to be alert against external as well as internal enemies posing a threat to the internal security of the country. Most of the big operations have the back up support of intelligence. We need to have defensive as well as offensive intelligence to forewarn, neutralize the impending threats and take proactive steps wherever required. We also need to have regular institutional framework to compile, collate and act on intelligence received from various agencies. Multi Agency Centre (MAC) has made a good beginning in this direction.

7. Border Management The country has land borders with six countries stretching nearly 15,000 kms. We have had wars on three sides of our land borders with China, Pakistan and East Pakistan (presently Bangladesh). We also had infiltration problems through Punjab and Kashmir borders, illegal immigration problems through Bangladesh and smuggling of weapons through Indo-Myanmar border. Kashmiri militants have been taking shelter in PoK while North-East extremists are taking shelter in Bangladesh, Bhutan and Myanmar. Therefore, we need to guard our land borders effectively to prevent infiltration by terrorists, illegal immigration, smuggling of weapons and drugs etc. Coastal security also needs special attention and we need to ensure that the roles of Navy, Coast Guard and Coastal Police are clearly defined and all of them work in harmony with each other.

8. Cyber Security The Snowden revelations (WikiLeaks) of 2013 have made it evident that future wars will not be traditional wars which are fought on land, water and air. In fact, it appears that cyber space will be the theatre of warfare in the 21st Century. Therefore, any solid doctrine on internal security needs to cover this front also. India has just made a beginning in this direction. We need to cover a lot of distance before we could say that we have a safe cyber space. In the coming chapters, we shall analyse in detail the various challenges to our internal security.

Probable Questions Based on this Chapter

1. What are the attributes of internal security? How is it different from external security?
2. Discuss the major challenges to internal security faced by the Indian state after independence.
3. What are the key elements of a comprehensive internal security doctrine?

CHAPTER 2

Terrorism—Role of External State and Non-State Actors

> ‘Terrorism may be defined as the planned, organised and systematic use of violence as a means of coercion for political or religious or ideological purposes.’

Terrorism has become a global phenomenon, but all attempts in the past for arriving at an internationally accepted definition of terrorism have proved futile. This ambivalence is primarily due to two reasons.

Firstly, a ‘terrorist’ in one country may be viewed as a ‘freedom fighter’ in another; secondly, it is known that some states encourage various criminal acts being carried out in another state. Hence, there is an obvious lack of political will to any universally acceptable definition of terrorism. Irrespective of these constraints, we can definitely say that:

> ‘Terrorism is a state of terror, panic and a fear psychosis, created by an individual or a group of people in order to force, coerce or blackmail the authorities, using violent methods to accept their demand or to attain political, religious or ideological goals.’

Terrorism is thought of as a method of war, which consists of intentionally attacking those who ought not to be attacked.

2.1 Classification of Terrorism

Terrorism can be classified into two categories—(i) terrorism by external state actors and (ii) terrorism by non-state actors.

2.1.1 Terrorism by External State Actors

When any Government directly or indirectly indulges in terrorism against its own people or the people of another country, it is referred to as terrorism by state actors.

Also, terrorism against another country, whether in support of international terrorism or in order to destabilise that country, can be classified as 'external state sponsored terrorism'

Terrorism in Kashmir is a direct manifestation of state policy of Pakistan and ISI influence, while hinterland terrorism by Indian Mujahidin or SIMI is indirectly supported by ISI and the state of Pakistan. *Therefore, Pakistan which is an external state actor is challenging India's internal security directly as well as indirectly.*

Similarly, time and again aspersions have been cast on the role of Bangladesh and Myanmar that they have played the role of external state actor regarding terrorism in north east.

Support to terrorism can be by various means, such as financial support to militant organisations, technical support, arms, training and infrastructural support, or ideological support.

2.1.2 Terrorism by Non-state Actors

In this case, the act of terrorism is performed by an individual or a group which is not associated with or financed by any Government. *Non-state actors have generally no direct or indirect link with any government or government agency while pursuing their agenda, though indirect linkages cannot be completely ruled out.* Naxalites, LTTE and North-east extremists are some examples of non-state actors.

Many important terrorist groups like *Lashkar-e-Taiba* (LeT) and Indian Mujahideen (IM) also claim to be non-state actors but have de facto support from Pakistan.

The use of non-state actors is essentially the employment of a proxy element, which gives the state of Pakistan a degree of deniability. However, there is no doubt that none of the so called 'non-state actors', like the LeT, could have operated with impunity without active funding, logistical and military support from Pakistan. The close linkages of the ISI and such groups are well documented as is their direct involvement in attacks like that of 26/11. These groups aim to not only create instability in states like Jammu and Kashmir, they also have a larger aim of destabilising the country. This is done through sporadic terrorist strikes, which spread terror and panic. This could also adversely affect the ability of the Indian state to pursue economic modernisation. The flooding of the country with counterfeit currency is also a way of weakening the economy.

Therefore, the so called 'non-state' actors operating from Pakistan are the proxies of the state, functioning under a clear charter of state policy.

Modus Operandi and Motto of ISI (Non-State Actors)

- To bleed India through thousand cuts
- To destabilise Indian economy through fake currency and other means
- To supply arms and explosives to all kinds of militants in India
- To take advantage of anti-Government groups operating within India and to provide financial, logistic and military support to such groups
- To spread and support Islamic fundamentalist activities
- To spread communal hatred and communal violence in India with the aim to divide and weaken the country.

2.2 Categorisation of Terrorism in India

Terrorism in India can be broadly classified into four major categories:

- Hinterland terrorism
- Jammu and Kashmir militancy
- North-East insurgency
- Left-Wing extremism

Out of these, the last two do not have direct linkages with non-state actors, so we will deal with them in separate chapters. Terrorism in Jammu and Kashmir is due to Kashmir's historical background. It has been dealt with in a separate chapter.

2.3 Growth of Hinterland Terrorism

Hinterland terrorism is the terrorism that is spread all across the hinterland of the country. Such terrorist acts have been taking place all over India without any specific reason. Yet, if we look back and analyse, there appears to be a sequential, well planned, well motivated growth of terrorism in India.

1. After failing in two conventional wars against India, especially post the humiliating defeat in 1971, Pakistan adopted the path of sub-conventional war/proxy war by supporting terrorist activities in India since the last three decades with the motto of 'bleeding India through thousand cuts'.
2. The seeds of present terrorism were sown in the Khalistan movement in Punjab in the eighties. This proved to be the most deadly terrorist movement in India. The evil design was to create a buffer sovereign state between J&K and rest of India.
3. After Punjab, Pakistan targeted Kashmir in the late eighties and tried to take advantage of anti-India separatist sentiments in a section of Kashmiri population, and it continues to do so, till date. Terrorism in Kashmir was basically operated by Pakistan occupied Kashmir (PoK) based Islamist terrorist organisations created, trained, inspired and directed by ISI, like LeT, JeM, Hizbul Mujahideen, etc.

4. In the meanwhile, SIMI was formed in Aligarh in 1977 with its motive to liberate Indian Muslims from western influence and make them follow Islamic code of conduct. In the 1980s and 1990s, SIMI became a highly militant and extremist group and took a more radical posture. Therefore, it was banned under Unlawful Activities Prevention Act (UAPA) in 2001.
5. The Ayodhya incidents of 1992 also saw the rise of reactionary terrorist activities all over India, especially in Mumbai (1993 Bombay serial blasts). This provided a big opportunity to ISI to carry forward its nefarious designs of spreading terrorism and communalism in India.
6. The 21st century saw the formation of Indian Mujahideen (IM) after the ban on SIMI. It was to project to the outside world that terrorism in India was a purely indigenous development, arising out of ill-treatment of Muslims and not sponsored from across the border. Doctored videos of Gujarat riots were used by ISI to mobilise, recruit and radicalise the youth.
7. The ISI has always tried to take advantage of communal incidents like the Ayodhya issue and the Gujarat riots for inciting young Indian Muslims. The increasing efforts of ISI to exploit communal sentiments have ensured that the Muslim community remains vulnerable to mobilisation, recruitment and radicalisation. In recent times, there were reports of Lashkar-e-Taiba recruiting young Muslims in riot affected Muzaffarnagar district.
8. We saw reactionary right wing extremist activities in 2006–07 in the form of bomb blasts in Malegaon, Mecca Masjid, Hyderabad, Ajmer Sharif and Samjhauta Express. Initially, investigating agencies of various state police had allegedly implicated innocent Muslim youth in these cases. This resulted in heavy resentment in Muslims and gave another boost to radicalization of Muslim Youth by ISI, LeT, SIMI and IM etc.
9. The Harkat-ul-Jihad-al-Islami (HUJI) of Bangladesh was also found involved in many terrorist attacks in India.

➤ 2.3.1 Important Terrorist Attacks in India

We can say that the last two decades have been marked by the presence of ISI sponsored terrorism in India's hinterland which was earlier confined to Punjab and J&K. Some of the more important incidents are mentioned below:

- Bomb blasts in Mumbai in 1993 that killed around 300 people
- Brahmaputra Mail train bombing in 1996 that killed 33 people
- 58 people killed and more than 200 injured in 1998 Coimbatore bombings, targeted at L. K. Advani in his election rally
- Air India Flight AI-814 hijacking in 1999 by Harkat-ul-Mujahideen with active support from Taliban
- Attack on Red Fort in 2000
- Attack on J&K Assembly in 2001
- Attack on Indian Parliament on 13th December, 2001 by Lashkar-e-Taiba and Jaish-e-Mohammed
- Attack on Akshardham temple in Gujarat in 2002 by Lashkar-e-Taiba and Jaish-e-Mohammed

- 68 people killed in four separate attacks in Mumbai in 2003
- 70 people killed in Delhi bombings two days before Diwali in 2005
- Blasts in Mumbai in 2006 killing 209 people by Lashkar-e-Taiba
- Malegaon blast by right wing extremists in 2006 killing 37 people
- Lucknow, Faizabad and Banaras attacks in court complexes in 2007 carried out by Indian Mujahideen
- Samjhauta Express and Ajmer Sharif Blasts by right wing extremists in 2007
- Attack on CRPF camp in Rampur in 2007
- Blasts in Jaipur, Bangalore, Ahmedabad and Delhi in 2008 carried out by Indian Mujahideen killing 115 people
- 171 people killed in terrorist attack by LeT in Mumbai in 2008, popularly known as 26/11
- German Bakery, Pune bomb blast in 2010 in which 17 people were killed
- 26 killed in serial bomb blasts by Indian Mujahideen (IM) in Mumbai in 2011
- Attack on Delhi High Court by IM in 2011 in which 12 people were killed
- Hyderabad bomb blasts in 2013 which killed 16 people by IM
- Bodh Gaya blasts in 2013 by IM
- Patna Election Rally blasts in 2014

Hence, it is evident that the terrorists have concentrated their target on India's political capital, financial capital, IT and scientific hubs, religious places and places of tourist interest.

Hinterland terrorism is also sometimes assisted by neighbouring countries through the borders; hence it can be referred to as *trans-national terrorism.* It is part of Pakistan's state policy after their defeat in 1971 war to bleed India through thousand cuts, given its obvious inability to take on India in a conventional war. Terrorists are provided training, infrastructure and weapons in Pakistan and then infiltrated into India through LoC or through Nepal.

➤ 2.3.2 Active Militant Outfits

Lashkar-e-Taiba (LeT) It is one of the largest and most active terrorist organisation in South Asia. It is operating mainly from Pakistan and Pak occupied Kashmir (PoK). It was founded in 1990 by Hafez Saeed. Lashkar-e-Taiba has attacked military and civilian targets in India. The 2001 attack on the Indian Parliament and the 2008 Mumbai attacks were also carried out by LeT.

Jaish-e-Mohammed (JeM) It was formed by Maulana Masood Azhar in March 2000 after a split within Harkat-ul-Mujahideen (HUM) shortly after his December 1999 release from prison in exchange for the passengers of Indian Airlines Flight IC 814 which was hijacked by HUM. A majority of members left HUM and followed Azhar into the newly founded group. JeM, in coordination with LeT, has been implicated in the 2001 Indian Parliament attack in New Delhi.

Hizbul Mujahideen It is a Kashmiri terrorist group founded in 1989. The current leader of the group is a Kashmiri known under the alias of Sayeed Salahudeen who usually resides in PoK.

Students Islamic Movement of India (SIMI) SIMI is a banned Islamic student organisation formed in 1977. Earlier, the stated mission of SIMI was 'liberation of India' from western materialistic cultural influence and to convert Muslims to live according to the Muslim code of conduct. But SIMI became militant and extremist in the backdrop of communal riots and violence between Hindu and Muslim groups in the 1980s and 1990s and took a more radical posture. Its motto became 'to convert whole of India into Islamic land'. SIMI was banned by the Indian government in 2001 when it was found to have indulged in terrorist activities.

Harkat-ul-Jihad-al-Islami (HUJI) It is a Pakistan and Bangladesh based very old Islamic terrorist organisation working in Pakistan, Bangladesh and India. HUJI has claimed responsibility for the 2006 Banaras bombing and 2011 Delhi bombing. HUJI had started its operations in Afghanistan after the Soviet retreat from the country. Its Bangladesh unit was formed in 2002. It is believed to be backed by Taliban.

Indian Mujahideen (IM) It is an Islamist terrorist group based In India, which has carried out several attacks against civilian targets in India. It was borne out of the ranks of SIMI. IM has reportedly taken responsibility for several blasts carried out in the last decade. Police investigations have revealed the group to be a front for the Pakistan based Lashkar-e-Taiba. In fact ISI, LeT and HUJI encouraged formation of IM in their effort to hide the involvement of Pakistan in terrorist activities in India and to project to the outside world that terrorism in India was an indigenous development arising out of maltreatment of Muslims. In 2010, IM was declared a terrorist organisation and banned by the Government of India. New Zealand, UK and US also declared it a terrorist organisation. Its ultimate aim is to create an 'Islamic caliphate' across South Asia. This organisation came into the limelight after the UP blasts of 2007 in the court premises in Lucknow, Varanasi and Faizabad. It recruits a wide range of disenchanted Muslims youths — from petty criminals to highly paid software professionals. Recently, one of its main leaders, Yaseen Bhatkal has been arrested by Indian security agencies.

Sleeper Cells A sleeper cell refers to a cell, or isolated grouping of sleeper agents, that lies dormant until it receives orders or decides to act. A sleeper agent is a spy who is placed in a target country or organisation, not to undertake an immediate mission, but rather to act as a potential asset if activated.

2.4 Reactionary Right-wing Terrorism

Hindu right wing organisations have been accused of involvement in terrorist attacks, including the Malegaon blasts, Mecca Masjid bombing (Hyderabad), Samjhauta Express bombings and the Ajmer Sharif dargah blast. This so called 'right wing terrorism' is supposed to have developed as a reaction to ISI sponsored terrorism and alleged Muslim appeasement by the Government of India. It tried to target Muslim dominated areas. These attacks have been allegedly carried out by a Pune based group 'Abhinav Bharat' headed by an Army officer Colonel Shrikant Purohit, Sadhvi Pragya and Swami Aseemanand.

All these incidents had taken place between 2006 and 2007. After 2007, no such incidence has come to light after the arrests were made. So it appears that this reactionary right wing terrorism was individualistic in nature rather than an organised movement involving multiple organisations.

2.5 Reasons for Spread of Terrorism

- More technology available to conduct acts of terror
- Targets of terrorism are more widespread than ever before
- Sophisticated means of communication (electronic media, print media, social media, internet) helped terrorists to quickly promote their ideology and hate campaign
- Intolerance in society due to increasing population and decreasing resources
- Increasing globalisation of the society
- International recognition and support to terrorist groups
- Links between terrorism and organised crime to earn easy money

2.6 Key Issues

2.6.1 How do the Terror Groups Fund Themselves? How do they Procure the Ammunition and Technology Required?

India faces different types of internal security threats. The groups involved raise funds from different sources, ranging from state sponsorship to fake currencies, to extortion and taxation, crime and smuggling, amongst others. Some cases are given below.

ISI Sponsored Terrorism

The militancy in J&K presents a classical case of state-sponsored and financed terrorism. The ISI employs state and private resources, like money from drugs and contraband, donations and charities, as well as the globalised network for raising and moving funds from Jehadi Islamic fundamentalists across the globe. This support is further augmented by funding from the Kashmiri diaspora and NGOs. These are thereafter used as part of Pakistan's proxy war against India, thereby bringing various components of funding together.

However, in the case of Indian Mujahideen (IM), state sponsorship in the form of financial support from ISI, mobilisation through organised criminal activities to raise funds and exploitation of globalised networks for financial resources have been the ways to keep their unlawful activities going.

It is believed that ISI's terror network is self-supporting financially and the money comes from:

- Donations from Islamic countries in the name of Jehad
- Earnings from drug trafficking
- Issuing fake Indian currency notes (FICN)
- Other kinds of organised crime

It is believed that the financial network operates through a few trusts, like the Al-Rashid from Karachi and the Rabita Trust from Islamabad. Usually these trusts operate through fake bank accounts.

The transfer of money to terrorist organisations is largely done through *hawala* transactions. Many a times, it has been found by Indian intelligence agencies that agencies like JeM, LeT and HM are funded indirectly by the ISI through the above mentioned means.

Funding Sources for Other Forms of Terrorism

Most insurgencies of the North-east receive funding from extortion and taxation, which is a local source. This is supplemented by trafficking of drugs, weapons and counterfeit currency. The insurgencies in the region have limited state-sponsored funding from outside and raising finances through private sources is the norm.

The case of CPI (Maoist) led insurgency is similar, with local financial resources providing the bulk of its funding. They also take a share from big infrastructure projects like roads, national highways, dams, rural development projects, etc. Apart from this, they receive security money from mining companies and multinational corporations (MNCs) operating in the country. But there is no substantive evidence of state sponsorship to naxalism. They have also not profited substantially from the globalised financial environment.

These groups then use the funds collected to smuggle weapons, explosives and technology based equipments, like satellite radios, from across the border. India has porous borders with Nepal, which is exploited. Similarly, borders with Bangladesh, Myanmar and Pakistan are often used for pushing in weapons and ammunition.

➤ 2.6.2 Institutional Framework to Tackle Terrorism

Before 2008, terrorism was fought mainly by the Intelligence Bureau (IB) with the help of state police and Central Armed Police Forces. The IB played the role of an intelligence agency which coordinated the efforts of various state police forces. The operations and investigations part were looked after by the state police. After the assassination of Indira Gandhi, a special commando force (NSG) was created to engage and neutralize the terrorist threats in specific situations. NSG commandos were trained in high risk tasks like counter hijacking and counter terrorist operations.

New Changes after 26/11

Although the Mumbai Police Force and the NSG are applauded for their operations during the 26/11 attacks, their initial response and operating procedures brought to light serious flaws in coordination. After the 26/11 Mumbai attacks, many steps were taken by the Govt. of India in this regard. The Government also announced the creation of many new institutions NIA, NATGRID, MAC (revamping), NCTC. Many steps were taken on the legal front also.

1. National Investigation Agency (NIA)

The National Investigation Agency (NIA) is a federal agency established by the Indian Government to combat terror in India. NIA has concurrent jurisdiction which empowers the Centre to probe terror attacks in any part of the country, covering offences, including challenges to the country's sovereignty and integrity, bomb blasts, hijacking of aircraft and ships, and attacks on nuclear installations. It also deals with counterfeit currency, human trafficking, narcotics or drugs, organised crime (extortion mobs and gangs), plane hijacking and violations of atomic energy Act and weapons of mass destruction Act.

NIA aims to be a thoroughly professional investigative agency matching the best in international standards. It aims to set the standards of excellence in counter terrorism and other national security related investigations at the national level by developing into a highly trained, partnership oriented workforce.

2. NATGRID

The National Intelligence Grid or NATGRID is an integrated intelligence grid that will link the databases of several departments and ministries of the Government of India so as to collect comprehensive patterns of intelligence that can be readily accessed by intelligence agencies. It is a counter terrorism measure that collects and collates a host of information from government databases including tax and bank account details, credit card transactions, visa and immigration records and itineraries of rail and air travel. This combined data will be made available to 11 central agencies, viz Research and Analysis Wing, the Intelligence Bureau, Central Bureau of Investigation, Financial intelligence unit, Central Board of Direct Taxes, Directorate of Revenue Intelligence, Enforcement Directorate, Narcotics Control Bureau, Central Board of Excise and Customs and the Directorate General of Central Excise Intelligence.

It is yet to become operational.

3. Revamping of Multi Agency Centre (MAC)

MAC is a multi-agency centre for Counter Terrorism whose mandate is to share terrorism related intelligence inputs on a day to day basis. Multi Agency Centre (MAC) was created at Delhi and Subsidiary Multi Agency Centres (SMACs) in various states comprising representatives from various security agencies for streamlining intelligence efforts after Kargil war. But it was revamped after 26/11. The Multi Agency Centre (MAC) in the Intelligence Bureau shares intelligence with various agencies that include police, CAPFs, defence and financial intelligence agencies. It also shares intelligence with SMACs established in various states and Union Territories through video-conferencing on a continuous and real time basis. Reciprocally, the other agencies are also obliged to share intelligence with the Multi Agency Centre.

The Centre operates on a 24 hour basis. It also acts as a Database in the form of National Memory Bank related to counter-terrorism intelligence. MAC has also been given additional responsibility of accounting and auditing of intelligence related to counter terrorism and enhancing the capacities of all the stakeholders in counter terrorism efforts.

Within a short span, MAC has proved its utility.

4. Creation of Four New NSG Hubs

The limitation of inadequate security forces was addressed by opening NSG hubs at four places at Mumbai, Kolkata, Chennai and Hyderabad other than Manesar in order to ensure faster and more effective reaction to crisis situations.

5. Coastal Security Scheme Revamped

The issue of maritime security and the lack of it surfaced and gained much attention after the Mumbai attacks. To strengthen coastal security of the country, series of measures have been taken to review, upgrade and strengthen the coastal security of the country. The following major decisions/initiatives have been taken by the Government :

- The task of guarding the Indian coastline right from the shoreline has been entrusted to the Coast Guard. However, the responsibility of overall maritime security rests with the Indian Navy.
- Coastal States/UTs have been directed to expedite the implementation of the approved Coastal Security Scheme such as early completion of construction of coastal police stations, check posts, out-posts etc.
- The coastal States and UTs have been directed to immediately start coastal patrolling by locally hired fishing boats/trawlers.
- The coastal States/UTs have been directed to carry out vulnerability/gap analysis on their coasts in consultation with Coast Guard.
- Ministry of Shipping, Road Transport and Highways has been directed to streamline the process of registration of all types of vessels, i.e., fishing as well as non-fishing vessels.
- To issue ID cards to all the fishermen and all the population in the coastal villages.

➤ 2.6.3 Legal Framework

The first special act to deal with terrorism was the Terrorist and Disruptive Activities (Prevention) Act or TADA as it is commonly called. It came into force after Indira Gandhi's assassination. But following allegations of its misuse, it was allowed to lapse in 1995 and another special act called the Prevention of Terrorism Act (POTA) was enacted in 2002 in the aftermath of the December 2001 attack on Parliament. POTA was also repealed in 2004. After the 26/11 Mumbai terrorist attack, the Unlawful Activities (Prevention) Act, UAPA Amendment Act came in force in December, 2008 which was further amended in 2012.

1. Terrorist and Disruptive Activities (Prevention) Act or TADA

TADA was an anti-terrorism law which was in force between 1985 and 1995 (modified in 1987) in the background of the Punjab insurgency and was applied to the whole of India. It was allowed to lapse in 1995 due to widespread allegations of abuse. It was the first anti-terrorism law legislated by the government to define and counter terrorist activities.

The law gave wide powers to law enforcement agencies for dealing with terrorist and 'socially disruptive' activities. The police were not obliged to produce a detainee before a judicial magistrate within 24 hours. The accused person could be detained up to one year without even filing a charge-sheet. Confession made to police officers was admissible as evidence in the court of law, with the burden of proof being on the accused to prove his innocence. Courts were set up exclusively to hear the cases under this Act. The trials could be held in camera with the identities of the witnesses kept hidden. Under 7A of the Act, Police officers were also empowered to attach the properties of the accused under this Act.

2. The Prevention of Terrorism Act, 2002 (POTA)

POTA was an anti-terrorism legislation enacted by the Parliament of India in 2002. The Act was enacted due to several terrorist attacks that took place in India especially the attack on the Parliament.

Analogous to the provisions contained in TADA, the law provided that a suspect could be detained for up to 180 days without filing of the charge-sheet in court. It also allowed law enforcement agencies to withhold the identities of witnesses, and to treat a confession made to the police as an admission of guilt. Under regular Indian law, a person can deny such confessions in court, but not under POTA. Also unlike TADA, it had no provision to allow preventive detention.

Changes after 26/11

Many relevant amendments were made to the already existing Unlawful Activities (Prevention) Act.

1. Unlawful Activities (Prevention) Act (UAPA) Amendment

UAPA is an act to provide for the more effective prevention of certain unlawful activities of individuals and associations (dealing with terrorist activities) and for matters connected therewith. UAPA was enacted in 1967 and amended in 1969, 1972, 1986, 2004, 2008 and 2012. With 2012 amendments, UAPA includes economic offences within the ambit of terror acts. Definition of "terrorist act" has been expanded to include offences that threaten the country's economic security, procurement of weapons, raising funds for terrorist activities and counterfeiting Indian currency. It also granted additional powers to courts to provide for attachment or forfeiture of property equivalent to the counterfeit Indian currency involved in the offence or to the value of the proceeds of terrorism involved in the offence.

2. NIA Act, 2008 and Special NIA Courts

The National Investigation Agency Act (NIA Act) was passed by Parliament in December 2008. As per the Act, NIA has concurrent jurisdiction which empowers the Centre to probe terror attacks in any part of the country, covering offences, including challenge to the country's sovereignty and integrity, bomb blasts, hijacking of aircraft and ships, and attacks on nuclear installations.

Other than offenses of terrorism, it also deals with counterfeit currency, human trafficking, narcotics or drugs, organised crime (extortion mobs and gangs), plane hijacking and violations of atomic energy act and weapons of mass destruction act.

Various Special Courts have been notified by the Central Government of India for trial of the cases registered at various police stations of NIA under Section 11 and 22 of the NIA Act 2008. Any question as to the jurisdiction of these courts is decided by the Central Government. These are presided over by a judge appointed by the Central Government on the recommendation of the Chief Justice of the High Court with jurisdiction in that region. The Supreme Court of India has also been empowered to transfer the cases from one special court to any other special court within or outside the state if the same is in the interest of justice in light of the prevailing circumstances in any particular state. They are empowered with all powers of the court of sessions under Code of Criminal Procedure, 1973 for trial of any offense.

The trials by these courts are held on a day-to-day basis on all working days and have precedence over the trial of any other case against the accused in any other court (not being a Special Court). An appeal from any judgment, sentence or order of a Special Court lies with the High Court. At present there are 38 Special NIA Courts. State Governments have also been empowered to appoint one or more such special courts in their states.

➤ 2.6.4 What is the Concept of National Counter Terrorism Centre (NCTC)? Is its Criticism Justified?

The concept was conceived after the 26/11 Mumbai attack, where several intelligence and operational failures revealed the need for federal agencies with real time intelligence inputs of actionable value, specifically to counter terrorist acts.

NCTC, conceived by the then Home Minister P Chidambaram, was mooted to be an apex body with single effective point of control for all counter terrorism measures. It was modelled on the lines of American and British bodies. NCTC was to be kept under the administrative control of IB.

The concept of NCTC faced criticism on the following points:

- As per the constitutional provisions, law and order is a state subject. The powers conferred on the NCTC to search, arrest individuals and carry out independent investigations without involving the State Government is viewed as an infringement on the states' powers and has raised a political storm.
- The principle of not granting the power of arrest to intelligence agencies has also been violated. This may lead to many operational problems for the intelligence agencies.

- The NCTC could be an ideal intelligence agency for handling all counter terrorism related intelligence. For this, we need a strategic planning body, investigations and an execution arm besides the intelligence outfit. However, a planning body needs to be separated from the execution agencies and each must be placed under an appropriate professional head.
- Where an operation is required to be launched to search, apprehend or arrest a militant, it would be prudent to incorporate the state police to get local help, including for navigation, translators, medical aid and handling of dead, wounded and other legal issues. Sustained investigations, including surveillance, would be difficult to carry out without the help of the local police.

Role of State Police in Prevention, Containment and Investigations can't be Ignored Prevention, containment and investigations leading to punishment are three distinct stages of counter terrorism. Prompt and actionable intelligence alone cannot prevent a terrorist attack. Effective policing, reliable technical infrastructure to monitor and counter a threat instantaneously and people's efforts are the other sides of the same coin. Hence, the questions: Who would do the policing or monitor the inputs from the technical infrastructure installed in an area? Who would integrate the efforts of the public? How would these be accomplished without the involvement of the local police and the state government?

The first person to reach the site of a terrorist attack would invariably be the local police. Once a terrorist attack happens, the resources needed to contain violence, manage the crowd and traffic besides preventing terrorist acts yet to be executed are beyond the capability of a central agency. Preservation of evidence, securing witnesses, managing the media and the relatives and friends of the deceased, etc. are other dimensions of the problem which can only be handled by the state police. Why should the states then not be part of the investigations?

The capability of the state police should be enhanced and intelligence, surveillance, sophisticated weapons, modern technologies and trained manpower should be augmented.

Unified Control and Effective Coordination with State Police For administrative efficiency, unified control is always better provided there is political unanimity on this. But, in a federal structure, it is not easy. It would be more prone to misuse, which would be dangerous for the country in the long term. So, this centralised agency should work in coordination with the state police and not independently.

Therefore, we can say that the centralised approach for NCTC is not acceptable to the states. Hence, we need a balanced approach with more local involvement.

2.7 Analysing the Level of Preparedness Against Terrorism

The four major roles of anti-terrorist agencies are:

- Intelligence gathering
- Training and operations

- Investigations
- Prosecution

The efficacy of each role has been analysed below:

➤ 2.7.1 Intelligence Gathering

This is presently being done by both the state police and the central government agencies. NATGRID and MAC, created after 26/11, have been vital additions. However, information and vital inputs from other government departments and non-government agencies, like financial transactions, passport and visa related crimes, cross-border infiltration, information relating to recovery of fake currencies, etc., still need to be streamlined, co-opted and factored in to facilitate the unveiling and investigation of a larger terror plot. We are in the process of achieving this goal after NATGRID becomes operational.

We also need to educate and train the civil society, media, corporate houses, hotels etc. which can provide further aid in the task of intelligence gathering. People's participation in preventing terrorist attacks is a vital area which needs careful thought and handling. A system to enable individuals of all age groups and sex to report information, including suspicious men or material, irrespective of how trivial they may be without any fear of harassment needs to be put in place. The police needs to be trained to act as partners of the public to control terrorism. There is need for a sustained campaign to educate people in this regard.

➤ 2.7.2 Training and Operations

The capability of the state police is limited as far as training and equipment are concerned. Central government agencies have started capacity building over the last five years. But there is scope for improvement.

As of now, for operations, IB plays the role of the coordinator with the police of different states but if operations need to be carried out simultaneously in many states, there is no unified command. Also, some states do not have the desired capability. Therefore, there is a need for a central agency to coordinate operations all over the country, but this agency should work in coordination with the state police and not independently. With creation of four more NSG hubs, we are in a better position for swift operations.

➤ 2.7.3 Investigations

Creation of NIA is a welcome step and it has been functioning well till now. There is scope for improvement in the investigating capabilities of the state police. Also, if one central agency investigates all cases of terrorism, which are inter-linked and may occur in different states, their investigation would be more efficient. This would help in the creation of a good data bank of various terrorist networks operating both inside and outside the country.

➤ 2.7.4 Prosecution

Our criminal justice system is very sluggish and a lot of time is spent in procedural aspects. There should be a time bound justice system. Special fast track courts should be established for quick disposal of terrorist cases. We need to improve a lot in this direction.

2.8 What More can be Done?

Dealing with the menace of terrorism would require a comprehensive strategy in which different stakeholders, i.e. the Government, political parties, security agencies, civil society and media would have an important role to play.

Political: A strong political consensus should be built in the country which says that national interest is supreme and, in national interest, many issues are non-negotiable. They should not be discussed in media or any other public platform. They should not be decided on vote-bank politics or party lines.

Legal: We need to have very stringent laws against terrorism and fast track courts which can deliver judgement within 3-4 months. Police has limited powers against terrorists and usually laws against terrorism are not very different from the laws against crime, for example, detention power is only 24 hours in both cases. Also, sometimes there is a need to carry out nationwide operations after the arrest of a terrorist which makes it difficult to produce the terrorist in the court within 24 hours. We need to evolve a process of criminal justice by which a terrorist can be tried and convicted within three to four months when the memory is fresh in the minds of the people. The loopholes in the justice system and delayed justice also emboldens the terrorists to indulge in violence. With stringent laws sealing all escape routes and delay options, even the families of individuals may serve as a restraining factor to prevent them from indulging in acts of terrorism.

Police: Strengthening the state police, enhancing their training capabilities and providing them with modern equipment for surveillance, investigation and operations is the need of the hour. We need to have modern scientific forensic laboratories. Also, special equipment against cybercrimes is needed because most of the terrorists operate through cyber network.

Media: The role of the media is also very crucial in the fight against terrorism. The media often indulges in needless debates on such issues which are of importance from the point of view of national security. In a democracy, debate is always welcome but on some issues, the media should take a more dispassionate view. For example, consider the issue whether SIMI should be banned or not. It is a clear matter of national policy and should be decided on the basis of national interest instead of debating in media. Similarly, many times the media and the intelligentsia discuss human rights of the terrorists while conveniently ignoring the human rights of the victims.

Public: The general public needs to be educated about the evil designs of our neighbouring countries. Both the majority and minority communities should promote interreligious harmony and work together for peace.

2.9 What is the Difference Between Terrorism, Insurgency and Naxalism?

The difference between terrorism, insurgency and naxalism has been defined below:

Terrorism: Terrorism is the planned, organised and systematic use of violence as a means of coercion for political, religious or ideological purposes.

This is a general term and as per the definition of terrorism, insurgency, militancy and naxalism are all different forms of terrorism.

Insurgency: It is defined as an act of rebellion and armed struggle by a section of society with a view to overthrow the government. The important factor here is that invariably, there is public support for the insurgents. The problems of Nagaland in the early fifties can be considered as a classical example of insurgency.

Naxalism: Naxalism refers to the use of violence to destabilise the state through communist' guerrillas warfare activities. Naxalism in India is mostly based on Maoist ideologies through which they want to overthrow the government by protracted people's war and install people's government.

Insurgency and naxalism are different forms of terrorism but all terrorism is not insurgency or naxalism.

Probable Questions Based on this Chapter

1. What do you understand by state actors and non-state actors in the context of terrorism?
2. What is the role of external state and non-state actors in creating challenges to internal security of India?
3. What are the main historical reasons for the presence of hinterland terrorism in India?
4. What are the main funding sources of various forms of terrorism in India?
5. Write a short note on NCTC.
6. What were the counter terrorism measures taken after 26/11 attack?
7. Who is Yaseen Bhatkal? Would you consider IM a purely non-state actor?
8. Invariably, identity crisis lies at the core of most forms of extremism. What are the various identity factors which fuel extremist tendencies in the Indian context?

CHAPTER 3

Jammu and Kashmir Militancy

3.1 Historical Background

Jammu and Kashmir was the largest princely state in 1947. Despite having nearly 77 percent Muslim population, it was ruled by a Hindu king, Maharaja Hari Singh. The state was known for pluralism and a culturally diverse society. There were five main regions:

- Province of Jammu, a Hindu dominated, largely plain area or low hills, bordering Punjab.
- To the north of Jammu, the Sunni Muslims dominated the Kashmir valley with a significant population of Hindu Kashmiri Pandits. The valley was one of the most beautiful parts of India with large number of tourists in summer. There was substantial Sikh presence in both Jammu Province and Kashmir valley.
- To the east of the valley, the hilly area of Ladakh was predominantly Buddhist with a slight presence of Shia Muslims. It shared borders with Tibet.
- The last two are the regions of Gilgit and Baltistan. These two regions were very thinly populated with mostly Shia Muslims. Gilgit and Baltistan shared borders with Afghanistan and Sinkiang province of China. It was also very close to the former Soviet Union. The geo-political location of the state of Jammu and Kashmir made it very crucial strategically.

➤ 3.1.1 Instrument of Accession and Referendum

On 15th August, 1947, fearing forced accession to India on one hand and communal backlash (due to dominance of Muslims) from Pakistan on the other, Maharaja Hari Singh did not accede to either India or Pakistan. He hoped for an independent, sovereign and completely neutral state. But the popular will of the people of Kashmir under the leadership of Sheikh Abdullah was to join India. Sheikh Abdullah consistently refuted the two-nation theory and he was perceived as a custodian of secularism in Kashmir. Hari Singh offered to sign a '*stand-still agreement*' with both countries which would allow free movement of people and goods across borders. Pakistan signed the agreement, but India said it would wait and watch. But relationship with Pakistan deteriorated soon when Pakistan suspended rail services between Sialkot and Jammu in September 1947. In October, while Sheikh Abdullah was leading a widespread agitation for complete transfer of power to the people in Kashmir, several Pathan tribesmen with the help of Pakistan Army invaded Kashmir.

The Maharaja asked Nehru for military help. Initially Nehru did not support accession without ascertaining the will of the people. But Mountbatten insisted that under international law, troops could be sent to Kashmir only after the state's formal accession to India. Sheikh Abdullah and Sardar Patel too insisted on accession. Finally, on 26th October, the Maharaja acceded to India by signing the '*Instrument of Accession*' and also agreed to appoint Abdullah as head of the state's administration.

As per this Instrument of Accession, except for Defence, Foreign Affairs, Finance and Communications, the Indian Parliament needs the State Government's concurrence for applying all other laws.

Even though both the National Conference and the Maharaja wanted firm and permanent accession, Nehru took a highly idealistic and controversial step by announcing that it would hold a referendum on the accession decision once peace and law and order had been restored in the Valley. This decision was taken to show India's commitment to democracy and to honour Mountbatten's advice.

The invaders were gradually driven out of the Valley except the area which is known as 'Pakistan Occupied Kashmir' (PoK) in India and 'Azad Kashmir' in Pakistan. Mountbatten suggested the Government of India to refer the Kashmir problem to the UN.

In 1951, the UN passed a resolution providing for a referendum under UN supervision after Pakistan had withdrawn its troops from the part of Kashmir under its control. The resolution has remained infructuous till date since Pakistan has refused to withdraw its forces from PoK. Plebiscite in Kashmir never took place. A UN Military Observer Group in India and Pakistan (UNMOGIP) still continues to supervise the ceasefire line and report the violation of ceasefire. **It is only for the state of Jammu and Kashmir that the accession of the state to India is still a matter of dispute between India and Pakistan and is still on the agenda of the UN Security Council.**

Since then, Kashmir has been the main obstacle in the path of friendly relations between India and Pakistan. India has regarded Kashmir's accession as final and irrevocable and Kashmir as its integral part. Pakistan continues to deny this claim and tries to raise the issue on international platforms while India says that it is a bilateral issue.

➤ 3.1.2 Line of Control

Withdrawal of Pakistani troops from the northern areas, collectively referred to as Pakistan occupied Kashmir (PoK) by India—and its reintegration with the rest of J&K had been the primary objective of India during the initial phase of the conflict. However, this objective slowly changed in a shift that became visible during and after the 1971 war with Pakistan. A *Line of Control* (LoC) was established after this war, and it is widely believed that during negotiations leading to the *'Shimla Agreement'* that followed the war, India and Pakistan agreed to convert this line into a permanent border between the two countries. Ever since, India's primary objective in the conflict of Kashmir has been to maintain the status quo and convert the LoC into an international border.

➤ 3.2 Kashmir Militancy — Low Intensity War or Proxy War by ISI

➤ 3.2.1 Beginning of Insurgency

After losing the initial battle in 1947 and the two main wars in 1965 and 1971, Pakistan resorted to the tactics of low intensity warfare as it realised that it could not win over India in a full scale direct war. It first supported the terrorist movement in Punjab and then started a separatist and militant insurgency in Kashmir in the late eighties. This low-intensity war between the two countries continues even today in the name of Jehad. It is a perpetual cause of worry to India.

In 1987, a disputed state election acted as a catalyst for the insurgency when it resulted in some of the state's legislative assembly members forming armed insurgent groups. In July 1988, a series of demonstrations, strikes and attacks took place. In 1989, a widespread popular and armed insurgency, supported tacitly from across the border, started which during the 1990s escalated into one of the most dangerous internal security issues in India.

It was the beginning of the mujahideen insurgency, which continues to this day. The insurgency was largely started by Afghan mujahadeen who entered the Kashmir valley following the end of the Soviet-Afghan war.

Initially, the already existing Jammu & Kashmir Liberation Front (JKLF) was used as part of this insurgency. It was created in 1964, reorganised in 1971 and was then used for the above purpose. The JKLF was the main insurgent Kashmiri group in the 1990s. Yasin Malik, a leader of the JKLF, was one of the Kashmiris to organise militancy in Kashmir. Its main demand was independence of Kashmir. *Since 1995, one faction of JKLF under the leadership of Yasin Malik has renounced the use of violence and calls for strictly peaceful methods to resolve the dispute.* But many new terrorist organisations have been leading the violent activities in the valley, like Hizbul Mujahideen, Lashker-e-Taiba, Jaish-e-Mohammed, Al-Badar, Harkat-ul-Ansar, Harkat-ul-Jehad-e-Islami (HuJi).

They infiltrated through the Line of Control. Pakistan's intelligence agency ISI and the government of Pakistan directly supported, funded and provided training, weapons, etc. to these terrorist organisations. This could be a well-planned ISI move to replicate the Punjab militancy model. These terrorist groups succeeded in ethnic cleansing of Kashmir by forcing nearly four lakh Kashmiri Pandits to flee the valley. Their properties and land were seized resulting in an acute demographic change in the Valley. The displaced Pandits, many of whom continue to live in temporary refugee camps in Jammu and Delhi, are still unable to return safely to their homeland. The government's inability to protect them has been one of the stark failures of successive governments.

On the other hand, many human rights organisations such as Amnesty International and the Human Rights Watch (HRW) regularly accuse Indian armed forces for human rights violations like 'extra-judicial executions', 'disappearances', torture and suppression of freedom of speech, etc. in Kashmir.

➤ 3.2.2 Present Status

The elections held in 2008 were generally regarded as fair by the United Nations High Commissioner for Refugees. They had a high voter turnout in spite of calls by militants for a boycott, and led to the pro-India Jammu and Kashmir National Conference forming the government in the state. The high voter turnout was seen as a sign that the people of Kashmir wanted peace and harmony.

There has been a change of strategy by the ISI in Kashmir in the last 4-5 years. Crowd mobilisation has been used as a tactic to defame Indian security forces and to internationalise the Kashmir issue. Stone pelting has become a routine feature of street protesters in Srinagar since the summer of 2008 when Amarnath land transfer became a hot issue for widespread agitation in the valley. Kashmiri teenagers have been involved in stone-pelting. There have been protest movements in Kashmir since 1989. Even a small incident is exaggerated by separatists for gaining political mileage. There was an increase in these incidents after Afzal Guru, the prime accused in the Parliament attack was hanged to death in Delhi in February 2013. Compared to 2012, there has been almost a six-fold increase in the number of times protesters resorted to stone-pelting on security forces in 2013. The number of security personnel injured in such incidents has increased more than three times. Fidayeen attacks re-emerged in 2013 after a lull of three years.

The turmoil in Jammu and Kashmir has resulted in thousands of deaths, but has become less deadly in recent years. There have been protest movements in Kashmir since 1989. The movements were created to voice Kashmir's disputes and grievances with the Indian government, specifically the Indian military.

➤ 3.2.3 What is Low Intensity War & Why was it Adopted by ISI?

Low intensity war is a long and protracted strategy to achieve a desired result, which cannot be achieved through direct war. It can be in the form of:

- Armed revolt
- Guerrilla warfare

- Political revolution
- National war of independence

➤ 3.2.4 Modus Operandi of the Proxy War in J&K

- To run a malicious campaign from Pakistan and PoK to mar India's image in print and electronic media
- To facilitate infiltration of terrorists from across the border and keep Indian security forces constantly engaged in fighting terrorists
- To attack the secular foundation of the state and support fundamentalist Islamic activities and ensure exodus of Hindus from the Valley
- To internationalise the Kashmir issue at every forum and paint India as persecutor of Muslims
- To increase terrorist activities in Muslim dominated districts of Jammu region
- To change the low intensity war to high intensity war at an appropriate time and term it as war of independence

➤ 3.3 Government of India's Development-Oriented Programmes in Kashmir

In 2004, Prime Minister Manmohan Singh had initiated a reconstruction plan (PMRP) with an outlay of ₹24,000 crore. This was mainly in infrastructure, power and transport. Some of the other schemes are as follows:

- Newly developed rail network to connect the Valley.
- The project 'UDAAN', an initiative of the Prime Minister, the National Skills Development Corporation and the Ministry of Home Affairs and industry, was started with the aim of providing skills to 40,000 youth over a period of five years.
- ₹900 crore worth road infrastructure development program in J&K on the lines of the Naxal-affected areas.
- Special scholarship scheme for Jammu and Kashmir to encourage the youth to pursue higher studies outside their state. The total cost of the scheme will be ₹1,200 crore.
- Project 'Umeed' for empowerment of women
- Project 'Himayat' for capacity building and employment of youth
- People-to-people contact with the rest of India through 'Bharat Darshan' programmes
- i) Capital investment subsidy @ 15% of the total investment in plant and machinery subject to ceiling of ₹30 lakh. However, MSMEs would be eligible for capital investment subsidy @ 30% of the investment of plant and machinery subject to ceiling of ₹3 crore and ₹1.5 crore for manufacturing and service sector, respectively, to all new and existing industrial units on their substantial expansion.

ii) 3% interest subsidy on the average of daily working capital loan to all new units for a period of 5 years from the date of commencement of commercial production.

iii) Central Comprehensive Insurance Subsidy Scheme with 100% reimbursement of premium to all new and existing units on their substantial expansion for a period of 5 years from the date of commencement of commercial production.

3.4 Key Issues

3.4.1 Should Article 370 be Removed or Amended?

Article 370 [C]

This article specifies that except for Defence, Foreign Affairs, Finance and Communications (matters specified in the instrument of accession), the Indian Parliament needs the State Government's concurrence for applying all other laws.

Thus, the state's residents live under a separate set of laws, including those related to citizenship, ownership of property and fundamental rights, as compared to other Indians.

The Government of India vide 1974 Indira-Sheikh accord committed itself to keeping the relationship between the Union and Jammu and Kashmir state within the ambit of this article.

The President may, by public notification, declare that this article shall cease to be operative or shall be operative only with such exceptions and modifications and from such date as he may notify, provided that the recommendation of the constituent assembly of the state shall be necessary before the President issues such a notification.

The 1974 Indira-Sheikh accord mentions that 'The State of Jammu and Kashmir which is a constituent unit of the Union of India, shall, in its relation with the Union, continue to be governed by Article 370 of the Constitution of India'.

Applicability of the Constitution of India to J&K

In exercise of the powers conferred by Clause (1) of Article 370 of the Constitution, the President, with the concurrence of the Government of the State of Jammu and Kashmir made the Constitution (Application to Jammu and Kashmir) Order, 1954, which came into force on 14th May, 1954.

Amendment of Article 370

Under Article 370(3), consent of state legislature and the constituent assembly of the state are also required to amend Article 370. Now the question arises, how can we amend Article 370 when the Constituent Assembly of the state no longer exists? Or, whether it can be amended at all? Some jurists say it can be amended by an amendment act under Article 368 of the Constitution and the amendment extended under Article 370(1). But it is still a moot question.

Demand for Abrogation of Article 370

Equally valid arguments are forwarded by those in favour of and against its abrogation.

Arguments in Favour The arguments in favour of Article 370 include:

- It has created certain psychological barriers and it is the root cause of all the problems in J&K.
- This Article encourages secessionist activities within J&K and other parts of the country.
- At the time of enactment, it was a temporary arrangement which was supposed to be repealed gradually.
- It acts as a constant reminder to the Muslims of J&K that they have still to merge with the country.

Arguments Against The arguments against abrogation of Article 370 include:

- Abrogation will have serious consequences. It will encourage secessionists to demand plebiscite which will lead to internationalisation of the issue of J&K.
- The contention of Article giving rise to secessionist activities is baseless as states like Assam and Punjab, which do not have any special status have experienced such problems.
- It would not only constitute a violation of the solemn undertaking given by India through the instrument of accession, but would also create unnecessary misgivings in the minds of the people of J&K, making the issue more sensitive.

Conclusion: It can be argued that abrogation of the Article is avoidable as it will certainly be raised internationally by Pakistan and it will give a chance to UN and the international community to intervene in J&K. So, maintaining the status-quo would be the best possible strategy as of now.

➤ 3.4.2 Should a Referendum be Done?

In the present scenario, a referendum will be meaningless as a lot has changed in the last 65 years, including the demography of Kashmir as about four lakh Kashmir pandits were displaced forcibly in the nineties. Pakistan has never withdrawn its troops from PoK, which was a pre-condition to the referendum. Therefore, India should not agree to the demand for referendum.

➤ 3.4.3 Why are there Frequent Ceasefire Violations by Pakistan?

Ceasefire violations are planned by the ISI mainly to keep the J&K issue alive, to try to internationalise it, keep the Indian forces engaged and to aid the infiltration of the terrorists into the Indian territory.

➤ 3.4.4 Should we Destroy Terrorist Training Camps in Pakistan?

This is a very sensitive issue. We should have complete intelligence about these camps and do surveillance to the extent possible. We should create a pressure on Pakistan to unilaterally destroy these training camps by giving ample proof. An attempt to destroy these camps from our side will be termed as war by Pakistan and it will surely internationalise the issue. Therefore, it would be better if we can mount diplomatic pressure on Pakistan to destroy such camps and stop abetting and aiding terrorism in India.

➤ 3.4.5 What Should be our Strategy Regarding the Rehabilitation and Resettlement of the Kashmiri Pandits?

Since Kashmiri pandits are original inhabitants of Kashmir since ages, they must be helped to get back to their motherland. We must create such a congenial atmosphere in Kashmir that these people would really want to go back.

Prime Minister Manmohan Singh in 2008 announced a special package for return and rehabilitation of Kashmiri migrants to the valley. The package includes housing, transit, accommodation, scholarship, employment and waiver of interest rates.

➤ 3.4.6 Should we Support Ladakh Demanding Union Territory (UT) Status and Jammu Demanding Separate State Within the Indian State?

Ladakh does need special status like many other undeveloped and remote areas. Similarly people of Jammu have a genuine grievance to some extent. But since all these were part of the state in 1947, their fate is interlinked. Any division of J&K will give Pakistan an opportunity to internationalise the issue which India wants to avoid. Therefore, we should take steps to ensure development of Jammu and Ladakh without bifurcating the state.

PROBABLE QUESTIONS BASED ON THIS CHAPTER

1. Write a short note on the instrument of accession of J&K with India.
2. What is the present political and security status of Jammu and Kashmir?
3. How has Pakistan's ISI changed its strategy regarding Kashmir in the last 5 years? Elaborate with suitable examples.
4. What is the modus operandi of ISI in aiding and abetting extremism in Kashmir?
5. What are the development initiatives taken by the central government in Kashmir?
6. What is Article 370? What will be the 'implications' of abolishing Article 370?

CHAPTER 4

Insurgency in the North-East

4.1 Historical Background of the North-East

4.1.1 Pre-Independence Era

There are more than 100 tribal groups in the entire north-east region of India. They have a rich cultural heritage with a variety of languages and customs. During the British era, they constituted an overwhelming majority of the population in most of the areas they inhabited. Non-tribals had not penetrated these areas to any significant extent. The British gave a special administrative status to these areas. The British government did not disturb their socio-political structure and followed a deliberate policy of excluding the outsiders. Outsiders were not allowed to acquire land in the tribal areas.

At the same time, the British government also supported the Christian missionaries to move in and establish schools, hospitals and churches. The missionaries introduced remarkable changes in the north-eastern society and modern progressive ideas prevailed amongst the tribal youth. It also helped the Britishers in keeping the nationalist (pro-independence) influence out of the tribal areas. This policy resulted in their isolation from the rest of India.

There was a virtual absence of any political, cultural, social, geographical, religious or business contact of the tribals in the North-east with the rest of India. So India's freedom struggle had very little impact on the tribals.

Thus, they never experienced the feeling of being part of a free country called India. Their main experience of outsiders was that of British officers and Christian missionaries only.

➤ 4.1.2 Post-Independence Era

After Independence, the Government of India focused on people-to-people contact and gave special attention to tribal policy. The Sixth Schedule of our Constitution is exclusively for this region and it provides for self-rule, autonomy and decentralization. Thus, district and regional councils were created.

Initially, there was only one state of Assam and one Union Territory, NEFA (North East Frontier Agency) covering the whole of the north-east. Later on, NEFA was named Arunachal Pradesh and granted the status of a separate state in 1987. While NEFA was developing comfortably and in harmony with the rest of the country, problems developed in other tribal areas which were part of Assam administratively.

In the mid-fifties, Phizo raised the banner of revolt in Nagaland and, later on, it spread to Mizoram, Manipur, Tripura and Meghalaya.

In 1960, Assamese was made the sole official language of the state. It led to an immediate and strong reaction in the tribal districts. Various political parties of the hill's tribal population began to feel alienated from Assamese and Bengali residents of the plains. The tribals were afraid of losing their identity and being assimilated by the policy of Assamization in government jobs and other professions, like doctors, traders, etc.

➤ 4.1.3 All Party Hill Leaders Conference

Representatives of hill areas merged into the All Party Hill Leaders Conference (APHLC) in 1960 and demanded a separate state within the Indian Union. APHLC fought elections and secured 11 out of 15 seats in Assam Legislative Assembly reserved for autonomous hill districts.

There were demonstrations and a major agitation developed. In the 1962 elections, an overwhelming majority of the Assembly seats from the tribal areas were won by the advocates of a separate state, who decided to boycott the State Assembly.

In 1969, Meghalaya was carved out of Assam as 'a state within a state' which had complete autonomy except for law and order, High Court, Public Service Commission and Governor. Finally, Meghalaya, Manipur and Tripura were granted statehood in 1972.

Meanwhile, secessionist movements developed in Nagaland and Mizoram. Nagaland was granted statehood in 1963 itself, while Mizoram became a state in 1987.

➤ 4.1.4 Present Situation of North-East Insurgency

The security situation in some of the north-eastern states has remained complex for a long time because of a number of militant outfits and their diverse demands. Assam, Manipur and Nagaland have continuously been a point of worry.

Lower Assam areas and KarbiAnglong regions are prone to ethnic and communal tension. The mistrust between tribals and non-tribals in Bodo areas has been growing. Garo insurgency in Meghalaya continues and Non-Manipuris are being targeted increasingly in Manipur.

Mizoram and Tripura have shown remarkable success in controlling insurgency and now they are largely peaceful for quite a long time. Government has signed ceasefire and Suspension of Operations (SoO) with most of the insurgent groups in the region. Government has steadily pursued the policy of dialogue and negotiations with any outfit which agrees to forgo the path of violence and come forward for peace-talks within the constitutional framework of India. In general the security situation in most of the north-eastern states has shown considerable improvement during the last five years.

Block year	Number of incidents	Number of terrorists killed	Number of security forces personnel killed	Number of civilians killed
1999–2004	8931	3099	884	3465
2005–2009	7045	2525	313	1930
2010–2013	3086	709	82	346
2014 (31.03.14)	200	38	04	36

➤ 4.2 State-wise Status

➤ 4.2.1 Nagaland

The first and the most significant insurgency started in Nagaland under the leadership of Phizo in the early 1950s.

The Nagas are the inhabitants of the Naga Hills in the eastern Himalayas, along the Burma border. Nagas consist of many tribes speaking different languages. After taking control over Assam in 1826, Britain steadily expanded its domain over Naga Hills by 1892.

During the British era, the Nagas were cut off from social and political developments in the rest of India. The British administered them with a soft iron as compared to their approach in the rest of the country. Outsiders were kept out. Their tribal culture and practices were not disturbed by the British administration. However, Christian missionaries successfully converted several tribes to Christianity. Due to continuous presence of Christian missionaries, Naga society is relatively more educated and aware than the other north-eastern states.

In April 1945, the Naga Hills District Tribal Council was established as a forum of the various Naga groups in the district. In February 1946, it was reorganized as a political organization called Naga National Council (NNC). NNC's objective was to work out the terms of relationship with the Government of India after the British withdrawal. NNC was against grouping of Assam in Bengal and wanted the Naga Hills District to be included in an autonomous Assam in independent India. It further emphasized local autonomy for the Naga Hills District, and a separate electorate for the Naga tribes.

Nine Point Agreement

After several rounds of negotiations, the Governor of Assam reached a Nine Point Agreement with the Naga leaders on June 26, 1947. It was decided that the Nagas would be granted judicial, executive and legislative powers, as well as autonomy in land-related matters. There was a ten years guarantee of these provisions at the end of which the Nagas could choose between extending the agreement or a new agreement. The Naga leaders were also promised unification of Naga territories from nearby districts into the Naga Hills District. However, the Constituent Assembly refused to ratify this accord. The Naga leaders envisaged a sovereign state with India as a 'guardian power' for ten years, while the Indian Constituent Assembly concluded that the Nine Point Agreement guaranteed only 'district autonomy within the Indian Constitution'.

Beginning of the Secessionist Movement

After independence, the Government of India started the integration of Naga areas with the state of Assam, and India as a whole. The hardliners led by A.Z. Phizo opposed this integration and rebelled under the banner of Naga National Council. Nagas demanded a separate sovereign state. They were also encouraged by some British officials and missionaries. In 1955, the separatists declared the formation of an independent government. They launched an armed rebellion. The Government of India sent the army to Nagaland in early 1956 to restore peace and order. By following a policy of suppression and non-negotiation, the government firmly opposed the secessionist demand for the independence of Naga areas.

On the other hand, the government also realized the need for reconciliation and winning over of the Naga people. As total physical suppression was neither possible nor desirable, the government followed a 'friendly approach' by encouraging the Nagas to integrate with the rest of the country in mind and spirit. The central government also made it clear that Nagas' right to maintain their autonomy in cultural and other matters would be respected by India.

Meanwhile, the Centre refused to negotiate with Phizo or any other separatists until they did not give up their demand for independence or armed rebellion. Simultaneously, it started negotiations with the more moderate, non-violent and non-secessionist Naga leaders headed by Dr Imkongliba Ao.

The armed rebellion was contained by the middle of 1957. Then the moderate Naga leaders under the leadership of Dr Imkongliba Ao negotiated with the Indian government for the creation of the state of Nagaland within the Indian Union. The Government of India accepted their demand through a prolonged negotiation and the state of Nagaland came into existence in 1963 as the 16th state of the Indian Union. This step not only strengthened national integrity and security but also restored people's faith in democratic values enshrined in our constitution. Non-violent means were seen with greater hope in the rest of India. Rebels lost their popular mass support. Though insurgency had been brought under control, sporadic guerrilla war was launched by Naga rebels in 1964 and it continues till date without any progress towards a political settlement. Instead, the present situation may be better understood as a very complex set of relations between a number of parties who have differing objectives, strategies, and capabilities. As a result, a precarious stability has been maintained over the last fifty years while cease-fire violations keep occurring routinely and almost continuously.

Major Terrorist Groups Operating in Nagaland

Nationalist Socialist Council of Nagaland (NSCN)—The Nationalist Socialist Council of Nagaland (NSCN) is a Naga nationalist group operating in Northeast India. The main aim of the organization is to establish a sovereign state, "Nagalim" unifying all the areas inhabited by the Naga people in Northeast India and Burma.

The National Socialist Council of Nagaland (NSCN) was formed in January, 1980 by Isak Chishi Swu, Thuingaleng Muivah and S.S. Khaplang opposing the Shillong Accord signed by the then Naga National Council (NNC) with the Government of India. Later, misunderstanding surfaced within the outfit leaders over the issue of commencing negotiation dialogue with the Indian Government and the NSCN split in 1980 into two factions; the NSCN-K led by S S Khaplang, and the NSCN-IM, led by Isak and Muivah. The split triggered a spate of violence and factional clash between the factions.

The objective of both the factions of NSCN was to establish a Sovereign State by unifying all the Naga-inhabited areas in the North East of India and Northern Burma which the organization and the people of the area proposed as Nagalim. Unification of all Naga tribes under one administration and 'liberating' Nagalim from India is listed as one of the main objectives of the organization.

Current Developments

- NSCN-Isiac Muviah (NSCN–IM) signed a ceasefire agreement with the Government of India in 2001, but insurgency continues by other groups
- Frequent ceasefire violations
- Presence of underground groups that deal in extortion, arms, drugs smuggling, etc.
- Clashes among different tribal groups, factions
- Tensions mainly between NSCN/K, NSCN/KK
- Public protest against underground activities of the rebels
- Parallel government

➤ 4.2.2 Manipur

The people of Manipur include the Meitei tribe, the Kuki tribe and the Naga tribe. Meitei forms about 60% of the total population. Meitei are Hindu tribes following Vaishnava tradition. Some of the Meitei are Muslims and Christians, too. Meiteis live in the plains, while Nagas and Kukis are in the hill districts.

A separatist insurgency began in 1964; Manipur was made a separate state in 1972. A more violent phase did not occur until 1978 when the separatists demanded secession from the Union of India on the ground of lack of development, plundering of local resources, and a general discontent. Alleged human rights violations by Indian security forces have only fuelled the insurgency.

There are currently 34 groups, including non-violent ones that demand independence from India. In 1999, some of these groups coalesced into an alliance organization called the Manipur People's Liberation Front. Of these, the three most prominent ones are the United National Liberation Front (UNLF), People's Revolutionary Party of Kangleipak (PREPAK), and People's Liberation Army (PLA) of Manipur. The UNLF is estimated to have 2,500 active militants, while the PREPAK has 1,500, and PLA 3,000. As of today, Manipur is the worst case scenario in the north-east as far as militancy is concerned. Apart from the fact that there are more militant groups in the state than anywhere else, the rivalry between these outfits often leads to greater violence.

The Kuki insurgent groups want a separate state for the Kukis to be carved out from the present state of Manipur. The Kuki insurgent groups are under two umbrella organizations, Kuki National Organization (KNO) and United Peoples Forum.

The situation is further complicated because insurgent groups are not united for the same cause. The Nagas wish to annex part of Manipur and merge with a greater Nagaland or Nagalim, which is in conflict with Meitei insurgents demands for the integrity of their vision of an independent state. There were many tensions between different tribes and the region has witnessed numerous clashes between Nagas and Kukis and Meiteis and Muslims.

Insurgent groups are demanding alternative arrangement, reintroduction of inner line permit to remove non-local population.

There is reported nexus between Maoist and Manipur insurgents; especially PLA blockade of the NH-37 highway is a usual feature due to continuous fight with Nagaland. PLA has assisted Maoists by imparting training to cadres and supplying weapons and communication equipment.

➤ 4.2.3 Mizoram

Among the ethnic and secessionist conflicts, the resolution of the Mizoram issue was a notable success. Armed insurrection had persisted in Mizoram for more than two decades. The movement by the Mizo National Front had racial and religious overtones, and its declared aim was secession of Mizoram from the Indian Union. There was an armed uprising in 1966 and violent conflict continued well into the 1980s. The Mizoram Accord of June 1986 succeeded in bringing the violent conflict of the past decades to a satisfactory conclusion. Three factors may be said to have contributed to this historic conflict resolution: firstly, Prime Minister Rajiv Gandhi's sincere and positive gestures were greatly appreciated by the people of Mizoram and its leaders, which laid the initial foundation for negotiations, secondly, the maturity of the two Mizo political personalities of the time, namely, the undisputed insurgent leader Pu Laldenga and the then Chief Minister Pu lal Thanhawala's unilateral offer of stepping down in favour of Laldenga as the chief minister and finally, the moderating influence and pressure of the Mizo civil society, especially the women who had been the most aggrieved and affected during the periods of violence.

In June 1986, the Government of India signed a peace agreement with Laldenga, leader of the Mizo National Front (MNF). By its terms, the MNF rebels laid down their arms and were granted amnesty against prosecution. The government agreed to grant full statehood to Mizoram, and Laldenga himself assumed office as chief minister, taking over from the Congress incumbent.

The model here was the Kashmir Agreement of 1975, when Sheikh Abdullah had returned to power in a similar fashion.

The agreement raised the prospect of the return of peace to the state of Mizoram.

The leaders of MNF made a spectacularly successful transition; once insurgents in the jungle, they are now politicians in the Secretariat put there by the ballot box. Peace brought its own dividend in the form of water pipelines, roads and, above all, schools. By 1999, Mizoram had overtaken Kerala as India's most literate state. The integration with the mainland is proceeding apace; Mizos are learning the official language, Hindi, and watching and playing the popular game, cricket. Since they also speak fluent English (the state's own official language); young Mizos, men as well as women, have found profitable employment in the growing service sector, in hotels and airlines in particular. Mizoram's chief minister, Zoramthanga, spoke of making his territory the 'Switzerland of the East'. In this vision, tourists would come from Europe and the Indian mainland while the economy would be further boosted by trade with neighbouring Burma and Bangladesh. The Mizos would supply these countries with fruits and vegetables and buy fish and chicken in exchange. Zoramthanga is also canvassing for a larger role in bringing about a settlement between the government and the Naga and Assamese rebels. It is easy to forget that this visionary had once been a radical separatist, seeking independence from India when serving as the defence minister and vice-president of the Mizo government-in-exile.

➤ 4.2.4 Meghalaya

Meghalaya is perhaps the least affected by insurgency in the north-east region. Problems in Meghalaya arise from the divide among various tribes as well as the divide between tribal and non-tribal settlers, identity issues and growing corruption, besides the sharp changes in demography due to Bangladeshi infiltrators. There is also fear of being reduced to minority by the native tribal population.

The main extremist groups operating in Meghalaya are:

Garo National Liberation Army (GNLA) GNLA aims to establish a separate Garoland for the Garo people. It was formed in 2009, and consists of 70 members, most of whom are ex-members of Achik National Volunteer Council (ANVC), Liberation of Achik Elite Force (LAEF) and National Democratic Front of Bodoland (NDFB). GNLA has been involved in extortion, attacks and bombings. Meghalaya has witnessed an upsurge in violence due to the activities of GNLA, remains the main active group in Meghalaya.

Achik National Volunteer Council (ANVC) ANVC was formed in 1995 with the intention of forming an Achik Land in the Garo Hills. As of now, a Suspension of Operations Agreement between the Government and ANVC has been in force since July 23, 2004.

Hynniewtrep National Liberation Council (HNLC) HNLC is a militant organization operating in Meghalaya. It was formed in 1992. It claims to be a representative of the Khasi-Jaintia tribal people, and its aim is to free Meghalaya from the alleged domination of the Garos and the non-tribal outsiders (the "Dkhars"). It was banned by the Centre in 2000.

Over the years, the HNLC built ties with the other secessionist organizations operating in north-east India, including the NSCN-IM of Nagaland, the NDFB of Assam and the National Liberation Front of Tripura (NLFT) and ULFA. The NSCN provided HNLC with moral, physical and financial support in its initial days. HNLC runs several businesses in Bangladesh.

The militant outfit Garo Hills Liberation Army, formed by deserting police personnel, have been launching guerrilla attacks against police and army personnel. Kidnapping and ransoms have become a norm in the western districts of the state. Extortion is being carried out by militants from the wealthy members of the state particularly, the coal barons. Also, ethnic tension is simmering between illegal immigrants from Bangladesh and the local indigenous tribal population. It is worth noting that these tensions are mainly due to ethnic issues and not related to religion. The clashes are between the locals and the illegal immigrants. However, criminal activities are a major concern. Trafficking of drugs like ganja, cocaine, opium, etc. is rampant as is smuggling of weapons, narcotics, black marketeering, etc. The state lies in a major smuggling route between Bangladesh and India.

➤ 4.2.5 Tripura

Tripura witnessed a surge in terrorist activities in the 1990s. The area under control of the Tripura Tribal Areas Autonomous District Council was increased after a tripartite agreement between New Delhi, the state government and the Council. The government has since brought the movement under control, and the government of Tripura has so far succeeded in limiting the extremist activities. There has been a steady decline in violence since 2003.

The evolution of insurgency in Tripura can be traced to the formation of the Tripura Upajati Juba Samiti (TUJS) in 1971, followed by the Tripura National

Volunteers (TNV) in 1981. The National Liberation Front of Tripura (NLFT) was formed on March 2, 1989 and its armed wing, the National Holy Army and All Tripura Tiger Force (ATTF) were formed in July 1990. NLFT seeks to secede from India and establish an independent Tripuri state. NLFT is currently proscribed as a terrorist organisation in India. The two outfits came up with secessionist agenda, disputed the merger of the kingdom of Tripura with the Indian Union, and demanded sovereignty for Tripura, along with deportation of illegal migrants, the implementation of the Tripura merger agreement and the restoration of land to the tribal people under the Tripura Land Reform Act, 1960.

Between 1990 and 1995, the insurgency remained low-key. But it grew in extent and magnitude between 1996 and 2004 and then started waning. The success of the insurgency during the initial stages was due to the advantages of the rough, rugged terrain, and the porous and extensive trans-border corridors with Bangladesh. Safe havens in Bangladesh, logistic support from the then supportive Bangladesh establishment and the external intelligence agencies based there, and networking with potential insurgent outfits aided it. A build-up of weapons, explosives and wireless communication systems, and extortion and 'levies', went into the making of the volatile insurgency.

This high voltage insurgency and an orgy of violence disrupted civic life and communications, and led to the closure of many educational and financial institutions, threatening the authority of the State. The state government took on the problems in a strategic and resolute manner under the sagacious and visionary leadership of Chief Minister Manik Sarkar. It formulated a multi-dimensional and fine-tuned strategy to respond creatively to the situation. The control mechanism was subsumed in counter-insurgency operations intent on swift area domination and ascendancy, as well as psychological operations and confidence building measures. An accelerated development thrust, management of the media, civic action programmes of the security forces, and the political process were additional factors.

Tripura scripted a story of triumph over insurgency and conflict-resolution, and demonstrated that insurgency was not an insurmountable phenomenon. What was needed to tackle it was a well-crafted, multi-dimensional strategy, resolute will, right vision and direction, honest and credible leadership, creative responses to the challenge and the growth and socio-economic-infrastructure dispensation to all sections of society. Also, the well calibrated and humane combat operations combined with psychological approach to the issues ensured that the local population was not alienated.

➤ 4.2.6 Arunachal Pradesh

The people of the three eastern districts of Arunachal Pradesh, namely Tirap, Changlang and Longding live in perpetual fear due to the presence of cadres of the two NSCN factions in the area, who resort to kidnapping, extortion and factional feuds. These three districts are part of NSCN-IM's projected State of Nagalim (Greater Nagaland).

Apart from these two Naga outfits, ULFA-I has strong presence in the region. ULFA-I cadres use the Lohit, Changlang and Tirap districts for infiltration into Myanmar, where the base camps of the outfit are located. The outfit uses these areas extensively for temporary transit camps while on the move as well as to escape counter insurgency operations in Assam.

Meanwhile, another emerging concern is the presence of CPI-Maoist cadres in the state. Movements of CPI-Maoist cadres had been reported from the Lohit and Lower Dibang Valley districts of Arunachal Pradesh.

The presence of the 53,000 strong Chakma and Hajong refugees in Arunachal Pradesh as well as influx of other foreigners, have also raised concerns among locals from time to time. According to All Arunachal Pradesh Student's Union (AAPSU) memorandum to President Pranab Mukherjee, 'The illegal settlement of Chakma and Hajong refugees has resulted in marginalization of indigenous tribes in the eastern-most part of Arunachal, while in the western part of the state, the Tibetans, Bhutanese and Nepalese are exerting their dominance over indigenous tribes and in central part of the state, there is a floating population of Bangladeshis which has created tension among various local tribes.'

Traditionally, the south-western districts of Tirap and Changlang, in the proximity of Nagaland, have been a happy hunting ground for both factions of the NSCN. While the Khaplang faction (NSCN-K) made its first inroads into the virgin territory in the early 1990s, the NSCN-IM faction soon made its move and carved out separate areas of influence in the district. In recent times, both the districts have witnessed occasional factional clashes between the outfits. Both outfits are known to run wide extortion network in these districts.

Arunachal Pradesh has also been used as a transit route by the ULFA. While the movement of the ULFA cadres between the eastern-most districts of Assam and the outfit's facilities in the Sagaing division in Myanmar through Arunachal Pradesh can be traced back to the late 1980s, the State's strategic importance for the ULFA has grown manifold after the outfit's December 2003 ouster from Bhutan, following a military crackdown. The outfit's dependence on its 28th battalion headquartered in Myanmar, for its hit and run activities in Assam, has become almost irreversible. There has, however, been a setback for the ULFA after two of the main strike units of the group's 28th battalion entered into a cease-fire agreement with the government in June 2008, diminishing the outfit's fire power to a great extent. ULFA cadres traversing the Assam, Arunachal Pradesh and Myanmar route had set up transit camps and safe houses in the Manabhum Reserve Forest spread over 1,500 square kilometres in the Lohit district.

➤ 4.2.7 Assam

After Nagaland, Assam is the most volatile state in the region. Beginning in 1979, the indigenous people of Assam demanded that the illegal immigrants who had emigrated from Bangladesh to Assam be detected and deported. The movement led by All Assam Students Union began non-violently with satyagraha, boycotts, picketing, and courting arrests.

Those protesting frequently came under police action. The election conducted in 1983 was opposed by the movement's leaders. The election led to widespread violence. The movement finally ended after its leaders signed an agreement (called the Assam Accord) with the central government on 15th August, 1985.

Under the provisions of this accord, anyone who entered the state illegally between January 1966 and March 1971 was allowed to remain but was disenfranchised for ten years, while those who entered after 1971 faced expulsion. A November 1985 amendment to the Indian citizenship law allows non-citizens who entered Assam between 1961 and 1971 to have all the rights of citizenship except the right to vote for a period of ten years.

There are several organizations that advocate the independence of Assam. The most prominent among these is the United Liberation Front of Asom (ULFA). Formed in 1979, the ULFA has two main goals: independence of Assam and establishment of socialist government.

The ULFA has carried out several terrorist attacks in the region targeting Indian military and non-combatants. The group assassinates political opponents, attacks police and other security forces, blasts railroad tracks, and attacks other infrastructure facilities. The ULFA is believed to have strong links with the NSCN and Naxalites.

It is also believed that they carry out most of their operations from the Kingdom of Bhutan. Because of ULFA's increased visibility, the Indian government outlawed the group in 1986 and declared Assam a troubled area. Under pressure from New Delhi, Bhutan carried a massive operation to drive out the ULFA militants from its territory.

Backed by the Indian Army, Thimphu was successful in killing more than a thousand insurgents and extraditing many more to India while sustaining very little casualties. The Indian military undertook several successful operations aimed at countering future ULFA terrorist attacks, but the organization continues to be active in the region. In 2004, ULFA targeted a public school in Assam, killing 19 children and 5 adults.

On 14 March, 2011, militants of the Ranjan Daimary led faction ambushed the BSF patrolling party on the way from Bangladoba in Chirang district of Assam to Ultapani in Kokrajhar, killing 8 jawans. Recently, Paresh Barua, leader of ULFA (anti-talks), has been arrested and sentenced to death in Bangladesh.

Of late, Maoists have been engaged in recruitment, training and extortion activities in upper Assam (Tinsukia and Dibrugarh) and Arunachal Pradesh.

The Central Government also gave special administrative autonomy to the Bodos in the state. However, the Bodos demanded a separate Bodoland, which led to a clash between the Bengalis, the Bodos, and the Indian military resulting in hundreds of deaths.

4.2.7.1 Bodoland Issue and the National Democratic Front of Bodoland (NDFB)

Bodos, the largest plains tribe of Assam started an armed struggle for a separate state in the mid-1980s. This armed struggle led to ethnic cleansing of the non-

Bodos along the north bank of the Brahmaputra. The Bodoland Autonomous Council (BAC) Accord was signed in 1993 and the Bodoland movement became more violent during the later part of the 1990s. In February 2003, the Bodoland Territorial Council (BTC) Accord was signed to end the one-and-a-half decade long Bodo movement. This was opposed by non-Bodos including Bengali speaking Muslims who have emigrated from Bangladesh. Non-Bodos allege that they have often been subjected to assaults, intimidations, killings, abductions and extortions by the Bodo militants and elements.

The heart of the Bodo problem is the ancient rivalry between the ancient Bodo tribes settled for ages on the northern banks of eastern Brahmaputra and the relatively recent arrival of Bengali-speaking immigrants. The Bodos speak their own language. There have been cycles of violence between the Bodos and the Bengalis who have migrated over years largely from Bangladesh and because of their agricultural skills taken over the Bodo lands slowly.

But the Bodos' demand for statehood had only distanced the non-Bodos from them. The creation of BTC in the face of a series of protests by non-Bodos is a pointer. The Bodos, who have already been outnumbered in BTAD, view the alarming rise in Muslim population – Bengali-speaking Muslims to be precise – as a potential threat. The Muslims are scattered partly on forest land and largely on the sandbars.

One of the negative fallouts of the present situation in the Bodo Territorial Areas District (BTAD) areas has been the idea of an exclusive 'ethnic territorial homeland'. The BTC, as an ethnically oriented territorial council, has failed to provide security to people other than the Bodos.

The Bodoland Territorial Council (BTC)

The 2008 violence against 'outsiders' occurred in the aftermath of the 2003 Bodo Accord which committed to safeguard Bodo language, land, socio-cultural rights, and ethnic identity. The Accord clearly stated that an autonomous self-governing body will be constituted, known as BTC within Assam in order to "fulfill the economic, educational, and linguistic aspirations and the preservation of land-rights socio-cultural and ethnic identity of the Bodos". Despite these provisions, the Bodos continue to feel insecure with regard to their land, ethnic identity and language vis-à-vis the minority communities.

The area under the BTC jurisdiction is called the Bodoland Territorial Area District (BTAD). BTC constitutes 70% of Non Bodo people who are against the creation of Bodoland. They are demanding cancelling villages having less than 50% Bodo people from BTC.

The BTAD consists of four new contiguous districts — Kokrajhar, Baksa, Udalguri and Chirang covering an area of 27,100 km^2 (35% of Assam).

The main provisions of the Memorandum of Settlement (MoS) relate 'to creation of the BTC, an autonomous self governing body within the State of Assam and under the provisions of the Sixth Schedule of the Constitution of India to fulfill economic, educational and linguistic aspirations, socio-cultural and ethnic identity of the Bodos; and to speed up the infrastructure development in BTC area'. The BTC comprises of 3,082 villages in four districts. The BTC has 40 elected representatives and the Assam Government would nominate six more. Of the elected representatives, 30 seats are reserved for tribals, five for non-tribals and the remaining five are open for general contest.

The National Democratic Front of Bodoland (NDFB)

NDFB is an armed separatist outfit which seeks to obtain a sovereign Bodoland for the Bodo people in Assam, India. It is designated as a terrorist organization by the Government of India. NDFB was formed in 1998. NDFB claims to be a representative of the Bodo people, who form around 10% of Assam's population. The main grievances of the group are the under-development in the region and the influx of immigrants. It aims to address these issues by seceding from India, and establishing a sovereign Bodoland.

The group carried out several attacks on civilians in Assam, targeting non-Bodo civilians as well as the security forces. In May 2005, it signed a ceasefire with the Government, but some of its factions continue to indulge in militancy. Recently in May, 2014 thirty-two people were killed, many others injured and thousands were rendered homeless in two districts of Assam after recent attacks by militants belonging to the anti-talks IK Songbijit faction of NDFB-S. The Assam government handed over the probe to NIA. It is allegedly the Bodos' fear of losing political clout that led to the latest wave of attacks on immigrants in BTAD in Assam.

4.2.7.2 Karbi Anglong Issue

Karbi Anglong district is the largest amongst the 27 administrative districts of Assam. Diphu town is the administrative headquarters of the district. Karbi Anglong is one of the country's 250 most backward districts (out of a total of 640). It is one of the eleven districts in Assam currently receiving funds from the Backward Regions Grant Fund Programme (BRGF). A number of indigenous people reside in this district. The Karbis are the most prominent amongst them. Other indigenous people residing in this district include the Dimasas, the Rengmas the Kukis, the Garos, the Tiwas, the Khasis, Hmars, the Mizos and the Chakmas.

There were violent clashes between the ethnic insurgent Karbi People's Liberation Tigers (KPLT) and the Rengma Naga Hills Protection Force (RNHPF) in Karbi Anglong district of Assam in December 2013 and January 2014. Over 3,000 people from the Karbi and Rengma Naga tribes were forced to leave their homes.

The KPLT is a breakaway faction of the ethnic insurgent KarbiLongri N.C. Hills Liberation Front (KLNLF). The KLNLF is demanding a separate State comprising two hill districts — KabriAnglong and DimaHasao. KLNLF is now engaged in talks with the Centre and the State government. When the KLNLF signed the Suspension of Operation agreement with the Centre and the Assam government, about 20 cadres of the outfit parted ways and formed the KPLT in 2010. The KPLT has been demanding the creation of self-ruled homeland for the Karbi people.

The RNHPF was formed in 2012 for protection of the RengmaNagas from KPLT attacks. The outfit has been demanding creation of a regional council for the RengmaNagas of KarbiAnglong.

4.3 Factors Responsible for Insurgency in the North-East

The factors responsible for insurgency in the North-east are given below:

- Feeling of alienation and deprivation among the tribal population
- Similar ethnicity across the border on Myanmar side
- Porocity of the border with Myanman due to difficult terrain
- Change in demographic pattern due to infiltration from across the border
- Disconnect with the other parts of India and fellow Indians
- Widespread corruption among the ruling elite
- Lack of visionary leadership among the tribal communities
- Lack of development and basic amenities
- Easy availability of arms and ammunition
- Political support from various factions
- Instability in Myanmar

Many of our neighbouring countries are being used by insurgent groups for shelter and training. Naga groups and Assam-based insurgency groups operate from Myanmar, militant groups of Meghalaya and Tripura from Bangladesh. Arms are also procured from across China. Their main source of funding is extortion and arms and drugs smuggling.

4.4 Government's Response to North-East Extremism

A composite strategy is being followed by the Government in the North East. It includes holding peace talks with those who abjure violence and dealing strictly with violent activities. Government has signed ceasefire and suspension of operations (SOO) with most of the insurgent groups (numbering 17-18) in the region. Government has steadily pursued the policy of talks / negotiations with any outfit, which agrees to forego the path of violence and come forward for peace talks within the constitutional framework of India.

The basic guiding principles of Government have been:

- Special Schemes for development for North-East
- Special packages for infrastructural development of North-East region
- Proportionate use of force
- Dialogue and negotiations
- Structural changes to give political autonomy
- Decentralisation and protection of tribal rights
- Improving road and rail connectivity in entire region
- Look East Policy viz-a-viz North-East region

- Business Summits to attract investment in North-East region
- Exhibitions and Seminars

Some of the major developmental initiatives taken for North-East region are:

- In October 1996, the then Prime Minister announced "New Initiatives for North Eastern Region" and stipulated that at least 10% of the Budget(s) of the Central Ministries/Department will be earmarked for the development of North Eastern States.
- The Government of India had decided to create the Non-Lapsable Central Pool of Resources for the North Eastern States and Sikkim from the year 1998-99onwards.
- The Department of Development of North Eastern Region (DoNER) was created in 2001 and was accorded the status of a full fledged ministry on May 2004. The ministry is mainly concerned with the creation of infrastructure for economic development of India's North-Eastern region.
- Special category status since 11th Plan: In order to mobilize financial resources, a policy decision was taken to earmark at least 10% of the Plan Budget(s) of the Central ministries/departments for development of the North Eastern states. And earmark at least 10% of the gross budgetary support (GBS) for the north-eastern states.
- In 1971, North Eastern Council was set up by an act of Parliament. It was restructured in 2002 as the regional planning body for the North Eastern Region.
- Social and Infrastructure Development Fund (SIDF) – Finance Minister's Package for NER, 2008-09
- Monitoring of mandatory expenditure of 10% of Gross Budgetary Support (GBS) for the North Eastern Region by the 51 non-exempted Central Ministries/Departments.
- Plan Scheme of 'Advocacy & Publicity' and Plan Scheme of 'Capacity Building & Technical Assistance (CB&TA)'
- Asian Development Bank assisted North East State Roads Investment Programme and World Bank assisted North East Rural Livelihood Project (NERLP)
- North East Industrial Investment and Promotion Policy, 2007
- Border Area Development Project (BADP)
- Hill Area Development Programme in the North East Region.

4.5 North-East Insurgents and their Foreign Links

The biggest foreign link of north-east insurgents are believed to be with Myanmar. India has a long international border shared by four states, Arunachal Pradesh, Nagaland, Manipur and Mizoram, with Myanmar. Difficult terrain and ethnic linkages of population on both sides of the border make it easy for the Indian insurgent groups / underground groups (IIGs / UGs) in the movement across the border as well as establishing camps, including training of fresh recruits, weapon procurement and their transfer to India.

Usually arms are procured from arms market in Thailand and finally brought to these four states.

The diplomatic and political initiative with the Myanmar government has yielded some results and Myanmar Government has signed a ceasefire agreement with NSCN (K) and given a deadline to METI insurgents of Manipur. But, because of their ethnic proximity and political compulsions, these groups have relocated themselves closer to the border which makes it easy for them to carry out attacks on Indian security forces.

With the cooperation of the Bangladesh Government, many IIGs (Indian insurgent groups) have been pushed out of Bangladesh. Therefore, these groups have now concentrated more in these four states.

➤ 4.5.1 Other North-eastern Neighbours

Apart from Myanmar, Bangladesh has been used by north-east insurgent groups as a hide-out, especially in Chittagong hills. However, after the takeover of the Sheikh Hasina Government, it is on the decline and many members of such groups have been arrested and handed over to India.

Nepal is being used as a hideout and transit to other countries adjoining China. Kathmandu airport is the transit point. Bhutan is also used by many of the Assam based underground groups like ULFA and NDFB. There are inputs which suggest moral support of the Chinese to the north-east insurgent groups.

➤ 4.6 Counter-Terrorism — Steps being Taken / Required

Multi-pronged approach is required.

- Communication and connectivity
- Infrastructure improvement
- Talks with insurgent groups
- Co-ordination between central forces and state forces resulting in a much better tactical response
- Stringent law and fast criminal justice system for quick disposal of terrorist attack cases
- Zero-tolerance policy towards violence
- Greater cultural interaction with the rest of the country
- Socio-economic development that includes a holistic inclusive development
- Presence of government to be felt everywhere
- Decentralization with alertness
- Improving administrative efficiency
- Pro-people governance
- Setting up High Courts in Manipur, Meghalaya and Tripura
- Coping up with regional aspirations

4.7 Key Issues

4.7.1 Feeling of Alienation / Racial Discrimination Amongst Residents of North-East

- They feel that they are not treated at par with other citizens of India.
- They feel that their culture is not promoted and properly highlighted in the right perspective in the rest of the country.
- They also feel that because of their distinct facial features they are compared to the Chinese and other similar ethnic communities. The recent murder of a north-east student in Delhi has again highlighted this sensitive issue. The government has seized the issue and has formed a special committee headed by an MP from the North-east to see how such discrimination can be avoided.

4.7.2 Should AFSPA (Armed Forces Special Power Act) be Repealed?

Although the Indian armed forces have been working in very arduous conditions but sometimes, due to stress, their behaviour also comes under the scanner. In the process, some innocent people may have suffered but the Army has also paid a heavy price through the loss of its soldiers and officers in guerrilla attacks.

There has been a long and continuous demand from the North-east that the special powers given to the armed forces in the Northeast and AFSPA should be withdrawn. Irom Sharmila Chanu has been on hunger strike for 10 years on this single issue.

It is true that, at times, security forces are accused of alleged human rights violations but with so many insurgent groups active in the whole of North East, the removal of AFSPA now is not advisable. If the armed forces are deployed without the power of search and seizure, then their deployment is meaningless. Therefore, there is a need to continue with AFSPA but the forces must also be wary of human rights violations and must be accountable for their actions and behaviour towards the public.

4.7.3 Bodo–Muslim Clashes of 2012

The Bodos have been fighting for separate Bodoland since 1986 under NDFB and ABSU. This was opposed by non-Bodos including Bengali speaking Muslims who have emigrated from Bangladesh.

In July 2012, there were communal clashes between Bodos and Muslims, which claimed many lives and displaced more than four lakh people. The violence initially started from Kokrajhar and Chirag and spread to all districts of Bodoland and lower Assam. Bodo organizations upped the ante on the illegal immigration issue demanding updating of citizens verification of Muslims and their citizenship status.

The violence in 2012 followed ethnic tensions between the indigenous Bodo people and Bengali-speaking Muslims. While the Muslims state that they are descendants of East Bengali Muslims brought to Assam during the British Raj, local communities allege that the Muslim population has increased, boosted by refugees from the erstwhile East Pakistan prior to the Indo-Pakistani War of 1971 and by subsequent illegal migration from Bangladesh.

The situation was further vitiated due to circulation of certain provocative SMSs, MMS and internet based messages triggering exodus of North-East people from the southern states of Andhra Pradesh, Tamil Nadu, Karnataka and Kerala under the fear of being attacked by Muslims.

As a counter to this, the Muslim students' organizations came together on one platform under United Muslims Front for People's Rights (UMFPR).

The situation was further vitiated due to circulation of certain provocative SMS, MMS and internet based messages triggering exodus of North-east people from the southern states of Andhra Pradesh, Tamil Nadu, Karnataka and Kerala under the fear of being attacked.

➤ 4.7.4 Exodus of Rohingya Muslims from Myanmar

Rohingya Muslims live in north of Rahine state of Myanmar and their population is about 8-9 lacs. They have not been recognised as citizens by Buddhist dominated Myanmar. They face persecution in Bangladesh and Thailand as well.

Bangladesh has refused them entry because

(i) Bangladesh is already overpopulated
(ii) Rohingya Muslims are a burden on the economy of Bangladesh
(iii) Bangladesh does not agree to the claim that Rohingyas are of Bangladeshi origin.
(iv) Bangladesh is already sheltering more than 3 lac Rohingya Muslims.

It is now trying to push them to India.

The exodus of Rohingya Muslims started after riots between ethnic Rakhine Buddhists and Rohingya Muslims in northern Rakhine state of Myanmar in June 2013. Violence between Muslims and Buddhists broke out again in late October. It resulted in at least 80 deaths, displacement of more than 20,000 people, and burning of thousands of homes. The outburst of fighting brought the total number of displaced since the beginning of the conflict to 1,00,000. Rohingyas have also suffered enforced segregation, are not allowed to leave their settlements, and are the subject of a campaign of commercial boycott led by Buddhist monks with serious threats against those who trade with Muslims. The UN has described the Rohingyas as among the 'world's most persecuted minorities'.

Over the past two years, the number of Rohingya Muslims coming into India has increased considerably. Most of them are reportedly taking shelter in Muslim-dominated areas in the country.

According to observers, the refugees have nothing in common with the Indian Muslims apart from their religion. Their way of life is completely different and hence they do not adjust too well over here.

The rising Buddhist-Muslim tensions originating in Myanmar are causing political repercussions at the regional level, raising India's security concerns.

It is a cause of worry for India that at least 1,500 Rohingya Muslims, escaping from the violence-prone Rakhine province, West Myanmar, are believed to have entered the country illegally. At least 20,000 'stateless' Rohingyas, unclaimed either by Myanmar or Bangladesh, have escaped in the aftermath of one-sided riots and other outbreaks of ethnic violence that left about 1,50,000 people displaced. It is believed that in 2013 alone, nearly 30,000-40,000 Rohingyas have infiltrated our country using the Bangladesh transit. The Bangladesh government has confirmed to New Delhi that terror groups like the Lashkar-e-Taiba (LeT) have instigated Rohingyas to avenge last year's sectarian violence in Myanmar.

The LeT is believed to be recruiting Rohingyas, offering to help them to seek revenge against the Buddhists through terrorist acts. The Union Home Ministry has decided to conduct a fresh census on the Rohingya Muslims following these reports.

LeT and Jamaat-ud-Dawah created an outfit known as Difa-e-Musalman Arakan [Burma]. This outfit was assigned to tie-up with Islamic organizations in Myanmar and Bangladesh. There are several other terror groups that are involved with the Rohingyas. While the Rohingyas are receiving funds from Saudi Arabia, weapons are apparently being sourced from Thailand.

There are sizeable Rohingya populations in Aligarh in Uttar Pradesh, in Andhra Pradesh, Maharashtra and even Jammu and Kashmir. Rohingya refugees are often seen protesting in Delhi outside the United Nations Human Rights Commission asking for UN refugee status. Our intelligence agencies have been on the alert ever since LeT supremo Hafiz Saeed issued a statement in Lahore accusing India of assisting the Myanmar regime in its persecution of the Rohingyas.

It is believed that the terror attack in and around Mahabodhi temple in Bodh Gaya on July 7, 2013, was targeted at international Buddhist tourists to avenge the killings of Rohingya Muslims in Myanmar.

With the arrest of 107 Rohingya Muslims over the past three months for illegally trying to enter West Bengal through Bangladesh, the Border Security Force (BSF) has taken up the matter with the Border Guards Bangladesh (BGB) and urged the BGB 'not to push them' into India.

Probable Questions Based on this Chapter

1. 'Invariably, identity crisis lies at the core of most forms of extremism in India's north-east.' What are the various identity factors which fuel extremist tendencies in the north-eastern states of India? What could be done to resolve the identity crisis?

2. How did a porous border with Myanmar give an impetus to insurgency in the North-east?
3. What are the main factors responsible for extremism in North-east?
4. How has the Government of India responded to insurgency in the North-east?
5. 'The continuation of AFSPA is a classic example of a Victorian era law to deal with modern era problem.' Discuss the circumstances which necessitate AFSPA and suggest changes in the Act to assuage people's sentiments.
6. Write a short note on each model that deals with the issue of extremism:
   a. Tripura Model
   b. Mizoram Model

CHAPTER 5

Left Wing Extremism

A War upon the State

➤ 5.1 What is Left Wing Extremism (LWE) or Naxalism (as it is popularly called)?

The term 'Naxal' derives its name from the village Naxalbari of district Darjeeling in West Bengal, where the movement originated in 1967 under the leadership of Charu Majumdar and Kanu Sanyal. It refers to the use of violence to destabilize the state through various communist guerrilla groups.

Naxalites are far-left radical communists who derive their political ideology from the teachings of Mao Zedong, a Chinese revolutionary leader. They have been operating in various parts of the country since the early seventies. At various points of time, different areas of the country have been seriously affected due to overt violence resorted to by naxalite groups active in those areas.

Former Prime Minister Manmohan Singh described naxalism as the most significant threat to internal security being faced by the country today. The threat has existed since long though there have been many ups and downs.

➤ 5.1.1 Philosophical background of Naxalism/Maoism/LWE

History has been witness to repeated occurrence of violence against the ruling elite mostly by the peasant class motivated by leftist ideologies. The ideological basis for these violent movements was provided by the writings of *Marx* and *Engels*. This ideology is commonly called **Communism/Marxism.** This was later supported by *Lenin* and *Mao Tse-tung* (Mao Zedong). Leftist ideologies believe that all existing social relations and state structures in an elitist/capitalist society are exploitative by nature and only a revolutionary change through violent means can end this exploitation. Marxism advocates removal of the capitalist bourgeois elements through a violent class struggle.

Maoism is a doctrine that teaches to capture State power through a combination of armed insurgency, mass mobilization and strategic alliances. Mao called this process, the 'Protracted Peoples War'. The Maoist ideology glorifies violence and, therefore, the 'bearing of arms is non-negotiable' as per the Maoist insurgency doctrine. Maoism fundamentally considers the industrial–rural divide as a major division exploited by capitalism. Maoism can also refer to the egalitarianism that was seen during Mao's era as opposed to the free-market ideology.

Maoism's political orientation emphasizes the 'revolutionary struggle of the vast majority of people against the exploiting classes and their state structures'. Its military strategies have involved guerrilla war tactics focused on surrounding the cities from the countryside, with heavy emphasis on political transformation through mass involvement of the lower classes of society. **'Political power grows out of the barrel of a gun'** is the key slogan of the Maoists. They mobilize large parts of the rural population to revolt against established institutions by engaging in guerrilla warfare. Maoism is no longer an ideological movement. Maoists are now creating a fear psychosis and denying democracy and development to tribals.

Unlike the political mass movements with violent underpinnings in the border areas, naxalites do not seek to secede from the Indian Union to establish a sovereign independent state of their own but their aim is to capture political power through armed struggle to install the so called 'people's government'.

➤ 5.1.2 Phases of Naxalism

Maoists spread their ideology very systematically and in a phased manner as follows—

1. **Preparatory Phase**—Detailed survey of new areas identifying important people, important public issues on which masses can be mobilised.
2. **Perspective Phase**—Mobilisation through frontal organisations – staging demonstration against government / administration based on local public grievances.
3. **Guerrilla Phase**—Converting the public movement into violent guerrilla warfare.
4. **Base Phase**—Here the Maoists try to establish their base and change the guerrilla zone into a liberated zone.
5. **Liberated Phase**—Establishment of people's Government.

5.2 Evolution of Naxalism in India

The spread and growth of Naxalism in India can broadly be divided into three phases or stages. The three stages have been described below.

5.2.1 First Stage

The Naxalite movement began in May 1967 in the three police station areas, Naxalbari, Khoribari and Phansidewa, of Darjeeling district in West Bengal. In November 1967, left wing extremists from the whole country founded the 'All India Coordination Committee' in Kolkata. In May 1968, the Committee was renamed as 'All India Coordination Committee of Communist Revolutionaries' (AICCCR). It declared four ideological aims:

1. Protracted people's war in accordance with Mao's teachings
2. Adapting to guerrilla warfare tactics
3. Establishment of rural revolutionary base areas
4. Encircling the cities as well as abstaining from parliamentary elections

AICCCR founded the revolutionary party CPI Marxist-Leninist (ML) in 1969 that was based on Maoist ideology. Soon, the Naxalite movement spread to many parts of the country, especially West Bengal, Odisha, Bihar and Andhra Pradesh. Their main followers were peasants and adivasis, or tribals, who often experienced discrimination and exploitation from state authorities. Also, several young unemployed people and students got attracted to the Naxal ideology. The period 1970 to mid-1971 was the peak period of violent activities by Naxalites. A joint operation of police and army in 1971 in the worst affected areas in West Bengal, Bihar and Odisha led to the arrest and death of almost all top leaders of the movement. Charu Mazumdar was caught and died in 1972 in police custody. The movement faced a severe blow during emergency when around 40,000 cadres were imprisoned in 1975.

5.2.2 Second Stage

The movement arose again in a more violent form after the Emergency. It continued to widen its base as per the strategy of 'protracted war'. Their base grew from West Bengal to Bihar to Odisha and also to Andhra Pradesh and Chhattisgarh. CPI(ML) was converted into People's War Group (PWG) in 1980 which had its base in Andhra Pradesh and struck heavy causalities among police personnel. PWG was banned by Andhra Government in 1992 but it continued its activities. Simultaneously, Maoist Communist Centre of India (MCCI) grew in strength in Bihar and carried out large scale attacks on landlords and other upper caste outfits. Naxal movement continued to grow at a steady pace across many parts of the country.

5.2.3 Third Stage

In a significant development in 2004, the People's War Group (PWG), operating in Andhra Pradesh, and the Maoist Communist Centre of India (MCCI),

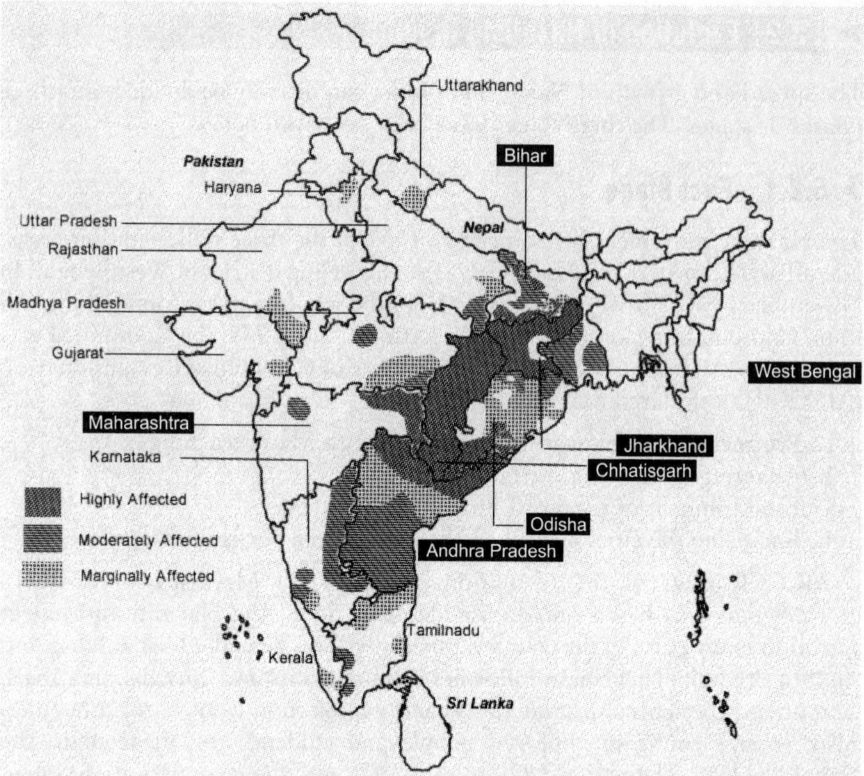

Extent of Spread of Naxalism

operating in Bihar and adjoining areas, merged to form the CPI (Maoist). Over 13 left wing extremist (LWE) groups are currently operating in the country. The CPI (Maoist) is the major left wing extremist outfit responsible for most incidents of violence and killing of civilians and security forces, and has been included in the Schedule of Terrorist Organizations along with all its formations and front organizations under the Unlawful Activities (Prevention) Act, 1967.

After the formation of CPI (Maoist), Naxal violence has been on the rise since 2005, to the extent that in 2006, the Prime Minister had to declare Naxalism the single biggest internal security challenge being faced by India. Estimated to be 40,000 strong, the Naxalites have been a strain on the country's security forces and a barrier to development in the vast mineral rich region in eastern India known as the 'Red Corridor'. It is a narrow but contiguous strip passing through Jharkhand, Chhattisgarh and Odisha. In fact, at the peak of Maoist movement in Nepal, Naxal influence was seen to be spreading from 'Tirupati to Pashupati'.

Today, the Naxalites influence a third of the geographical spread of country. Right now, the movement has expanded its activities covering over 460 police stations in 223 districts across 20 states. But the worst affected areas of the Maoist influence include approximately 30 districts of 7 states namely Chhattisgarh, Odisha, Maharashtra, Andhra Pradesh, Jharkhand, Bihar and West Bengal. Most of these areas fall in the Dandakaranya Region which includes areas of Chhattisgarh, Odisha, Maharashtra and Andhra Pradesh. CPI (Maoist) has stationed some battalions in the Dandakaranya region. Local panchayat leaders are often forced to resign and the Maoists hold regular Jan Adalat. They have been running a parallel government and parallel judiciary in these areas.

But violence alone cannot be the only yardstick to measure Maoist expansion. Maoists are also expanding in terms of indoctrination and consolidation. They are also trying to spread their ideology in the Bheel and Gond tribes dominated area, the 'Golden Corridor' stretching from Pune to Ahmedabad. They are trying to exploit new areas, various social groups and marginalized sections like Dalits and minorities through active association with their grievances against the state. Maoists have also made their presence felt in western Odisha, Upper Assam and Lohit in Arunachal Pradesh while they faced huge setbacks in Jangalmahal area of West Bengal and Kaimur and Rohtas districts of Bihar.

The movement's capacity to challenge the state has also increased enormously considering the incidents of violence and casualties resulting from them. The biggest incident was when they ambushed a whole CRPF Company in April 2010 in Dantewada of Chhattisgarh and killed 76 CRPF armed personnel, showing the extent of their strategic planning, skills and armament.

In 2013, the left wing extremist movement made international headlines when they killed 27 people, including some high-level politicians, in Sukma District of Chhattisgarh.

5.3 Party Structure

CPI (Maoist) is the main party now after the merger of various Naxalite groups in 2004. M Laxman Rao / Ganpati is the Secretary General of the party. The organizational structure of CPI (Maoist) is as follows:

It operates through Peoples Liberation Guerrilla Army (PLGA). PLGA has three kinds of force:

1. Basic force (Gathering of intellectuals)
2. Secondary force (Area committee plus guerrilla squads)
3. Main force (Structured on battalion/platoon format like the armed forces, and an intelligence unit)

As on date, the strength of PLGA is around 8,000-9,000 while Jan Militia is around 38,000. Usually 40-50 % of the total cadres consist of females.

5.4 | Aims and Objectives and *Modus Operandi* of the Naxalites

The aim of the naxalites is to destroy the legitimacy of the State and to create a mass base, with a certain degree of acceptability. The ultimate objective is to attain political power by violent means and establish what they envisage as 'The India People's Democratic Federal Republic'. The naxalites predominantly attack the police and their establishments. They also attack certain types of infrastructure, like rail and road transport and power transmission, and also forcibly oppose execution of development works, like critical road construction. Naxalite activity is also manifesting itself through various civil society and front organizations on issues such as SEZ policy, land reforms, land acquisition, displacement, etc., with the objective of expanding their mass base and acquiring support of some intellectual elite.

While impeding development works and challenging State authority, the naxalites simultaneously try to derive benefit from the overall underdevelopment and sub-normal functioning of field institutions like police stations, tehsils, development blocks, schools, primary health centres and anganwadi centres, which administer and provide services at the ground level and also reflect the State presence and writ.

5.4.1 Frontal Organizations of LWE (Left Wing Extremists)

The Maoists use their front organizations, like the Revolutionary Democratic Front, Peoples Democratic Front of India, Democratic Student Union and other student groups from left wing institutions like the Jawaharlal Nehru University (JNU) of Delhi, to generate people's sympathy through persistent pursuance of propaganda on issues of human rights violations by the security forces. Maoists take help from left leaning civil society groups, human rights groups, national and international media and other students groups for mass mobilization. They exploit the sluggish judicial system to get away from legal conviction and punishment.

5.4.2 Guerrilla Warfare

The Maoists use guerrilla warfare tactics. Guerrilla warfare is a form of irregular warfare in which a small group of combatants, such as armed civilians or irregulars, use military tactics including ambushes, sabotage, raids, petty warfare, hit-and-run tactics, and extraordinary mobility to fight a larger and less mobile traditional army.

➤ 5.4.3 Powerful Propaganda Machinery

Naxalites have very powerful propaganda machinery which is active in all major towns as well as in the national capital. They even have their supporters in the media. These NGOs and activists wage a non-stop propaganda war against any government step that aims to check the naxalite movement. As a matter of strategy, naxalites try to be on the right side of the media all the time. They have their sympathizers everywhere who raise a hue and cry in the name of human rights against police action on the Maoists. These media groups are conveniently silent when naxalites kill innocent people.

➤ 5.4.4 Tactical Counter Offensive Campaign (TCOC)

Maoists carry out violent activities called "Tactical Counter Offensive Campaign" (TCOC) which runs from March to early Monsoon in July. Maoists usually resort to TCOC every year to put the security forces in disarray so that they can go on a recruitment drive. The aim of "TCOC" is to exhibit and consolidate their (Maoists) strength, by carrying out violent operations. Going by the past experience, the rebels have launched a number of deadly attacks against security forces during the TCOC period.

➤ 5.4.5 Fresh Strategy of Maoists

Fresh strategy of Maoists is to expand outside forests into urban area, win over non-peasant classes and other social groups, seize leadership of ongoing local struggles, intensify mine warfare, militarise the Jan Militia, force the dispersal of police resources by launching attacks outside its strongholds, establish organisational bases in towns adjoining guerrilla zones and harden its stance downtrodden on abductions.

➤ 5.5 Links with Other Terrorist Organizations and Foreign Countries

The CPI (Maoist) has close fraternal ties with many north-east insurgent groups, especially the RPF/PLA of Manipur and National Socialist Council of Nagaland (NSCN-IM) for sourcing arms. Most of these outfits have linkages with external forces inimical to India. The CPI (Maoist) has also frequently expressed their solidarity with the Jammu and Kashmir terrorist groups. These ties are part of their 'strategic united front' against the Indian State. The CPI (Maoist) also has close links with foreign Maoist organizations in Philippines (Communist Party of Philippines), Turkey, etc.

The above outfit is also a member of the 'Coordination Committee of Maoist Parties and Organizations of South Asia' (CCOMPOSA), which includes ten

Maoist groups from Bangladesh, India, Nepal and Sri Lanka. The CCOMPOSA cited its chief aim as resisting not only US imperialism and globalization, but also the 'centralized' Indian state and its internal repression of minority people. It also targeted the alleged expansionist designs of India in South Asia backed by US imperialism. In 2006, CCOMPOSA at its Fourth Conference in Nepal reiterated its anti-India stand and reaffirmed its commitment to spread protracted people's war to capture state power through violent means in South Asia.

➤ 5.5.1 Sources of Funding and Linkages with Organized Crime

The main source of funding of the left wing extremist movements is extortion from government projects as well as from corporate companies working in their areas of influence. Most of the time, it is in the form of protection money. Sometimes they resort to kidnapping and killings also to terrorize the rich people so that they give financial help easily. Left wing extremism is most intense precisely in areas which are rich in natural mineral resources, i.e. where coal, iron, bauxite, manganese, nickel, and copper are found in abunda Odisha and Jharkhand alone account for more than half of the country reserves. Coal is by far India's largest energy resource. Therefore, it provi them enough scope for extortion.

➤ 5.6 Naxalites are not Really the Messiahs of the Downtrodden

From their ideology, it appears that naxalites are fighting for the rights of poor people and want to establish a people's government, while the facts are quite contrary. Social uplifting of the down trodden is not their real aim, rather it is political power. They study the local problems and issues and use them as fodder to foster their end game which is clearly the seizure of power through violent means.

Maoists have vested interest in keeping poverty alive because it enables them to expand their territory. They don't allow district administration to do any development work like building roads and improving electricity and water supply in the areas. The local population very soon realizes that they have been used by the naxalites and their social and economic issues take a back seat while the battle for supremacy emerges as the prime motto of the Maoists. But, at times, it is too late and the locals are forced to support them.

➤ 5.7 Factors Responsible for Rise of Naxalism

It is ironical that even after 66 years of Independence, many remote areas which are otherwise rich in mineral resources are yet to see any sign of development. This situation, combined with many other socio-economic problems, has contributed towards the rise of naxalism in India. These factors can be broadly categorized as follows:

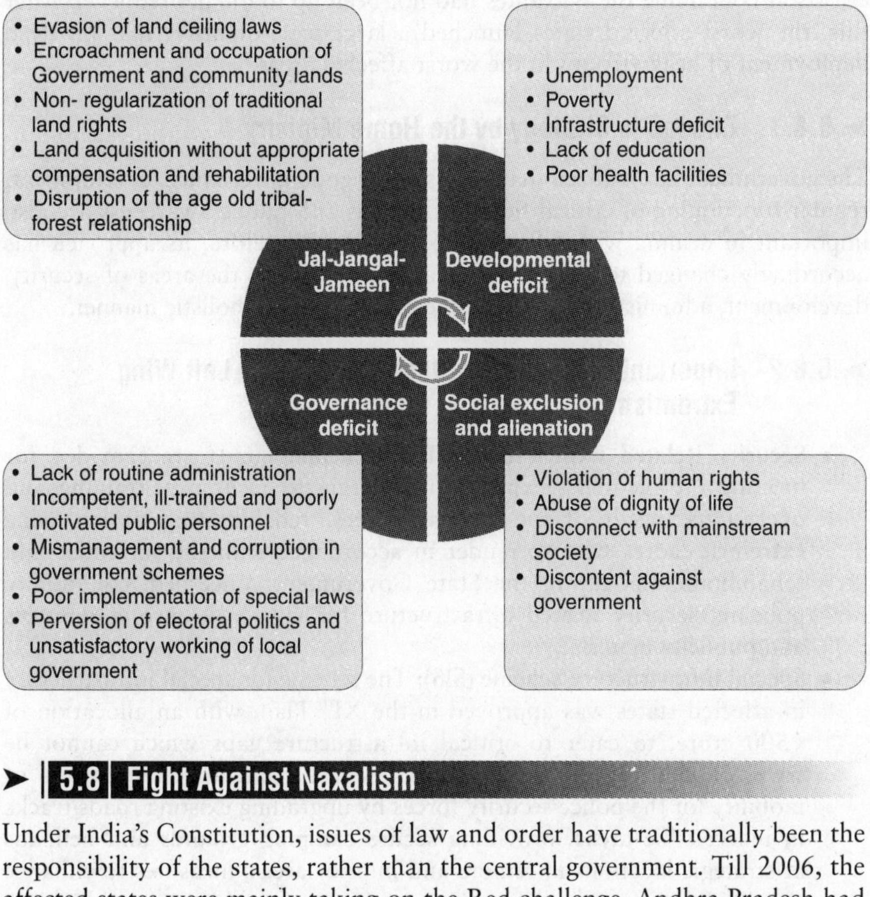

5.8 Fight Against Naxalism

Under India's Constitution, issues of law and order have traditionally been the responsibility of the states, rather than the central government. Till 2006, the affected states were mainly taking on the Red challenge. Andhra Pradesh had even succeeded in curbing naxalism to a large extent.

In 2006, after the Prime Minister's declaration of the naxal problem as the biggest challenge to internal security, many new steps were taken. This included creation of a separate division in the Home Ministry (Naxal management division) and appointment of an expert committee headed by D Bandopadhyay by the Planning Commission in 2006.

The expert committee underscored the social, political, economic and cultural discrimination faced by the scheduled castes/scheduled tribes (SCs/STs) across the country. The committee established the lack of empowerment of local communities as the main reason for the spread of naxalism. It further stated that state bureaucracy had failed miserably in delivering good governance in naxal affected areas. It recommended a tribal friendly land acquisition and rehabilitation policy.

More than three years after identifying Naxalism as the biggest internal threat, Prime Minister Manmohan Singh admitted in 2009 that the government's efforts at containing the Naxalites had not been up to the desired level. After this, the worst affected states launched a large-scale offensive that involved deployment of heavy troops in the worst affected areas.

➤ 5.8.1 Change in Strategy by the Home Ministry

The government has realized that the issues of good governance, development, regular functioning of critical field institutions and public awareness are also important in dealing with left wing extremism. Therefore, its approach has accordingly changed to deal with naxalite activities in the areas of security, development, administration and public perception in a holistic manner.

➤ 5.8.2 Important Schemes for States Affected by Left Wing Extremism

- **Security Related Expenditure (SRE) Scheme:** Funds are provided for meeting the recurring expenditure relating to insurance, training and operational needs of the security forces, rehabilitation of left wing extremist cadres who surrender in accordance with the surrender and rehabilitation policy of the State Government concerned, community policing, security related infrastructure for village defence committees and publicity material.
- **Special Infrastructure Scheme (SIS):** The scheme for special infrastructure in affected states was approved in the XIth Plan, with an allocation of ₹500 crore, to cater to critical infrastructure gaps which cannot be covered under the existing schemes. These relate to requirements of mobility for the police/security forces by upgrading existing roads/tracks in inaccessible areas, providing secure camping grounds and helipads at strategic locations in remote and interior areas, measures to enhance security in respect of police stations/outposts located in vulnerable areas, etc. Now, this scheme has been expanded to provide funds for upgradation of infrastructure, weaponry, equipment and training of special forces of the states affected by extremism.
- **Central scheme for assistance to civilian victims/family of victims of terrorist, communal and naxal violence:** This scheme was started in 2009. The broad aim of the scheme is to assist families of victims of terrorist, communal and naxal violence. An amount of ₹3 lakh is given to the affected families under the scheme.
- **Integrated Action Plan (IAP):** Planning Commission is implementing a plan for 88 selected tribal and backward districts in the country for accelerated development. The aim of this initiative is to provide public infrastructure and services. Existing model of spending ₹30 crore per district through a district level three-member committee headed by the District Magistrate, with the Superintendent of Police and the District

Forest Officer as members of the committee is being implemented. Major works/projects taken up under the IAP include construction of school buildings/school furniture, anganwadi centres, drinking water facilities, rural roads, panchayat bhawan/community halls, godowns/PDS shops, livelihood activities, skill development/trainings, minor irrigation works, electric lighting, health centres, etc.

- **Road Requirement Plan for extremist affected areas:** Phase I of the plan was approved in February, 2009 for improvement of road connectivity in 34 districts in 8 states extremely affected by left wing extremism, viz. Andhra Pradesh, Bihar, Chhattisgarh, Jharkhand, Madhya Pradesh, Maharashtra, Odisha and Uttar Pradesh, with a projected cost of ₹7,300 crore.
- **Scheme of Fortified Police Stations:** The Ministry has sanctioned 400 police stations in 9 affected states at a cost of ₹2 crore per police station.
- **Civic Action Programme (CAPs):** Under this scheme, financial grants are sanctioned to CAPs to undertake development in the affected states. This is a successful scheme which aims to build bridges between the local population and the security forces.

  Meanwhile, the Home Ministry has brought some changes in its civic action programme. It has now adopted an 'individual-oriented' approach rather than a 'project-oriented' approach as this will help in bridging the gap between locals and security personnel more efficiently. Under the project christened 'Winning Hearts and Minds', the Central Reserve Police Force and the Border Security Force, who have till now been spending funds on small projects and development activities which included building small bridges and roads, implementing drinking water and irrigation schemes, etc., can now spend ₹20 crore per annum, on welfare activities directed at individuals and families under the revised guidelines.
- **Roshani Scheme (Ministry of Rural Development):** It is a placement linked skill development scheme targeting 50,000 rural men and women, mostly the tribal population, in 24 worst affected districts. It emphasizes on special efforts to proactively cover the particularly vulnerable tribal groups (PVTGs) on a priority basis.

➤ 5.8.3 Administrative Hurdles in Dealing with Left Wing Extremism

1. Poor infrastructure, lack of communication and shortage of trained manpower are key problems in fighting with Maoists.
2. Due to lack of infrastructural growth, there is clear absence of routine administration in these areas which allows Maoists to run camps, collect taxes and extort money from all industries and infrastructure companies working in their area. Thus, Maoists conduct a virtual parallel government. The Dandakaranya region straddles different states. It gives the Maoists a distinct advantage.
3. Interstate boundaries are fissures which are being exploited by Maoists. There is poor coordination among various state police forces. The interstate trijunctions are the worst affected.

4. There is also lack of professionalism and proper understanding between central forces and state police.
5. Differences in policies of state governments regarding surrenders, talks and policing strategy are also exploited by the Maoists. Pressure in one state allows easy movement into another. It happened during Operation Greyhound which was very successful in Andhra Pradesh. It had almost eliminated Naxalites in the state but they made an easy escape to adjoining states like Chhattisgarh, Maharashtra and Odisha. Had the operation been supported by all these states at that time, naxalism would at least have been eliminated in the Dandakaranya region.
6. Besides this, since many rebels are recruited from among the tribals, they have a built-in advantage over the security forces. Even though government forces outnumber the rebels and have greater resources at their disposal, they frequently fall prey to devastating attacks in remote areas.
7. The state police is poorly equipped and trained and is short of manpower, while the central forces apparently lack commitment and motivation.

5.9 The Way Forward

Naxalism is not merely a law and order issue. The phenomenon of naxalism is directly related to under-development. It is not a coincidence that the tribal areas are the main battleground of left wing extremism today. Exploitation, artificially depressed wages, inadequate employment opportunities, lack of access to resources, under-developed agriculture, geographical isolation, lack of land reforms, all contribute significantly to the growth of the naxalite movement. All these factors have to be taken into consideration as we evolve solutions for facing the challenge. History tells us that masses do not want to associate with non-violent people. They are generally peace loving. It is only due to circumstances that they are forced to adopt a path of violence.

Naxalism is not the problem; rather it is the symptom of a problem. Why doesn't Naxalism flourish in the markets of Gujarat, the fields of Punjab or in the IT parks of Gurgaon and Hyderabad? Why is Maoist ideology succeeding in Nepal when it is failing in China? The answer is obvious. In the places that left wing extremism succeeds, people are relatively poor, they face oppression from various segments of society, and the government is indifferent to their plight with little prospects of things getting better in the future. Left wing extremism fails when the reverse is true.

To eliminate naxalism, it is not enough to eliminate their leaders, imprison their rank and file or arrange for mass surrenders of men and weapons. You do all of that and you can still fail; new leaders will rise, the cadres will return and weapons are easy enough to get.

To truly eliminate naxalism, we must undercut their *raison d'être*, their reason for existence. While their methods may be abhorrent, most of their goals (apart from overthrowing the government) are not. Therefore, the government must fulfil their goals for them. If they have nothing to fight for, they will not fight.

Electricity and running water are virtually non-existent in remote areas of the Red Corridor. The absence of basic necessities has produced opportunities for the naxalites to provide services to local residents, such as irrigation systems. The infrastructure that does exist has long been a target of the naxalites: power plants, schools, and phone and rail lines have all been attacked. This gives credence to the central government's assertion that security needs to be established before development can come. This is a contentious issue among affected states, which argue that the naxalites would be able to attract fewer new recruits if basic needs are met on a more acceptable basis.

The fight against naxalism has to be long and persistent. There must be multi-pronged composite strategy to deal with it. Developmental initiatives should follow security forces' action closely. Otherwise, success of security operations will not sustain for long.

We can broadly divide the strategy as follows:

➤ 5.9.1 Development Strategy

The following steps should be taken to wean away the masses from the influence of naxalism:

1. Special focus on political security and accelerated socio-economic development in a holistic manner
2. Better infrastructure like roads, electricity and communication in core naxal areas
3. Political parties must strengthen their cadre base in naxal areas so that potential youth can be weaned away from the path of naxal ideology
4. Affirmative action by state
5. Decentralization and participative democracy
6. Coordination among different departments of state to ensure holistic development
7. Coordination between police and different state departments
8. Coordination and implementation of schemes of different central ministries, especially the Integrated Action Plan for 82 districts and Road Requirement Plan for 34 districts.
9. Coordination and implementation of various development schemes, flagship programmes and distribution of titles under the Scheduled Tribes and other Traditional Forest Dwellers (Recognition of Forest Rights) Act, 2006, in left wing extremism affected states.

➤ 5.9.2 Security Strategy

Those who are hardcore ideologues and whose only purpose is to overthrow the state have to be dealt sternly with the policy of bullet-for-bullet. We have to wean away peace loving common people from the hardcore naxalites as these people do not want development. They use underdevelopment and governance deficit as a means to achieve their selfish goals. Operation Greyhound of Andhra Pradesh has shown a professional way to handle the naxal menace.

Some broad points of security strategy are given as follows:

1. Professional dominance by security forces
2. Primacy of state police at all levels augmented state police strength, upgradation and capacity building of local state police
3. Increasing the number of security forces in the strongholds of the Naxals
4. Local police infrastructure should be developed with more thanas, chowkis, posts and battalions. Thanas and chowkis should be strategically located and well-functional
5. Modernization of weapons and technical equipment
6. Improvement of communication systems and electronic surveillance systems
7. Special training to police personnel
8. Formation of specially trained special task forces on the pattern of the Greyhounds in Andhra Pradesh
9. Special emphasis on strengthening of local intelligence units of the affected states
10. Since it is an inter-state problem, the states should adopt a collective approach and pursue a coordinated response to counter it
11. Promote local resistance groups on lines of 'village defence committees' (VDC) in Jammu and Kashmir
12. Inter-state police coordination, especially in Dandakaranya region
13. Better command, control and coordination between state and central forces
14. Tightening of control on availability of explosives
15. Posting of competent and motivated police officers in LWE affected areas and subsequent incentives for choice postings and suitable reward packages.

➤ 5.9.3 Psychological Operations

The following measures should be implemented:

1. Effective and persistent psychological operations must be launched to delegitimize the movement
2. Media and public perception management
3. Administration to engage with public at large, civil society, NGOs to restore people's faith and confidence in the government machinery

➤ 5.9.4 Other Measures

The following measures should additionally be implemented:

1. Cutting financial support to the naxal movement
2. The doors for peace talks should always be open
3. There should be genuine attempt to win the hearts and minds of the people

4. Time-bound conviction of arrested cadre must be ensured through vital reforms in criminal justice system
5. Effective surrender and rehabilitation policy ensuring proper afety and care of their families
6. Better adherence to the law legislated for protection and development of tribals

➤ 5.9.5 A Few Success Stories in the Fight Against Naxalism

1. Story of Sandesh (Bihar)

Sandesh block in Bihar has seen gradual elimination of Naxalites. Sandesh comes under Bhojpur district. There are 11 panchayats under the block. A grassroots' view of the end of naxal dominance in panchayats of Sandesh block would be illuminating. Naxalism in Bihar started from two blocks of Bihar. Sandesh was one of them. The other adjoining block was Sahar. The most important factor which proved instrumental in dismantling naxal dominance was the Panchayat elections initiated in Bihar. In the panchayat elections of the year 2000, six panchayats had Maoist mukhiyas. The second panchayat elections were held in 2006. It was the first important signal of the growing unpopularity of Maoists in the villages. It also created a significant distance between the Maoist leaders and the local community. The process of social cohesion against the Maoists started in many panchayats of Sandesh block. This new attitude of the social order forced sympathizers of naxalites to mend their ways or leave the villages. Social pressure forced many naxalites to switch over to farming and shed off their association with naxal outfits. Gradually, Sandesh block grew relatively free from naxal violence.

2. The Aasdwar Project in Jehanabad (Bihar)

There are many initiatives started by the Bihar government to curb naxal movement in Jehanabad district which remained in the news for naxal violence for more than two decades. One such is the Aasdwar Project in Jehanabad district. The scheme is currently underway in five Naxalite affected panchayats of the district. These are Sikariya, Sewanan, Mandebigha, Surungpur-Bhawanichak and Jamuk, all in Sadar block. Villages under these five panchayats are witnessing a flurry of development activities on a war footing. The state government has come out with a liberal package of welfare schemes under Aasdwar, including construction of cement lanes, drains, chaupals and link roads worth ₹29 crore. Other works include construction of buildings for schools and Aanganwadi centres, culverts and individual toilets. The government has also taken some affirmative action in respect of forest rights (Forest Act 2008), displacement (R&R Policy), livelihoods (NREGA), etc. The people, at large, seem to have embraced the state's Aasdwar programme in a big way. So, as this case study amplifies, Naxalism can be defeated and eliminated by the process of development and a new social order but the change has to come from within.

3. AP Greyhounds Model

Andhra Pradesh had shown a model for controlling naxalism. Though the 'Greyhounds' naxal fighting force was its main element, infrastructure development and effective surrender and rehabilitation policy have also proved effective. The model was so successful that all the Naxalite leaders were forced to leave Andhra Pradesh and try new hideouts in Odisha, Chhattisgarh and Maharashtra.

Key elements in the Andhra Pradesh model

- Effective surrender and rehabilitation policy
- Culture of police leadership
- Infrastructure development
- Sound knowledge of local terrain
- Grass roots involvement in anti-Naxal operations
- Incentives to police for good work
- Superior intelligence, coordination and assessment
- Operations based on local intelligence

5.10 Key Issues

5.10.1 Intellectual Support to Naxalism

Top intellectuals like Arundhati Roy and Binayak Sen regularly support naxalism in the name of advocating an egalitarian society, human rights and tribal rights. They condemn security forces for human rights violation but surprisingly they adopt a noble silence when naxalites brutally kill security forces, politicians and common people. It clearly reflects their double standards. They should also understand use of violent means cannot be supported to achieve a noble cause in a democratic set-up. Although it has become a disturbing fact that resorting to violent agitation is the preferred strategy for aggrieved citizens to articulate their grievances as compared to constitutional methods of democratic agitation, the success of the Anna Hazare movement and subsequent electoral results in Delhi have proved otherwise. Rather than supporting Naxals blindly, these intellectuals should encourage Naxals to fight elections, to join mainstream society and to learn the art of give and take of democratic bargaining without aggression.

5.10.2 What was Saiwa Judum and why it Failed?

Salwa Judum was a movement in the Bastar area of Chhattisgarh which assumed the form of mass movement against the atrocities committed by naxalites. It literally means 'collective problem solving platform' and it gained momentum because people got fed up with naxalites' intimidation and extortion. The administration claims that it was spontaneous, peaceful and a voluntary case of public uprising against the Maoist movement. The naxalites never wanted the Salwa Judum movement to succeed in Bastar because they were hounded by the 'Greyhounds' force of Andhra Pradesh and Bastar was their biggest bastion. They established their people's government in Dandakaranya Zone (which is a cluster in the remotest corner of the five adjoining states of Chattisgarh, Odisha, Andhra Pradesh, Madhya Pradesh and Maharashtra). This is an area of immense strategic and geo-political importance for naxalites. They adopted some counter strategies against Salwa Judum. Firstly, the leadership of this movement was branded anti-people and some key leaders were executed. Secondly, the entire propaganda machinery in favour of the naxalites was ordered to throttle Salwa Judum movement in its infancy. Soon, the movement was discredited on many counts. It was shown that it was a proxy police movement and the police was recruiting children forcibly. It is believed that in 2006, more than 100 villagers involved in the movement were killed by the naxalites. Finally, in May 2013, senior Congress leader Mahendra Karma, who had supported the movement, was killed mercilessly. Surprisingly, the so-called human rights activists and intellectual supporters of naxalites were silent on this killing. With no support from any quarter to counter this propaganda, the Salwa Judum movement was killed in its infancy.

➤ 5.10.3 2013 Chhattisgarh Elections

For the first time in decades, the Maoists have encouraged calibrated polling in some areas, instead of fanatically implementing a policy to boycott the election. The districts of Chhattisgarh partially controlled by Maoists — with 12 Assembly constituencies — voted overwhelmingly in 2013. Compared to 2008, voter turnout in 2013 increased by 9.67 percentage points in 12 constituencies. The record rise in polling illustrates that Naxal-dominated constituencies embraced the democratic process more avidly than the rest of Chhattisgarh. The rise in polling in south Chhattisgarh was attributed to a reduction in Maoist strength. Several villages located deep inside Maoist areas voted overwhelmingly

It is believed that Maoists are fading in Chhattisgarh. A decreasing number of ambushes conducted on the forces, contradictory statements from rebel leaders indicating fissures in the rank and file are signs of this. Also, the large-scale desertion of cadres in some areas, increasing frequency and intensity of security operations in base areas hitherto unexplored by the forces and the initiation of welfare programmes in Bastar division have pushed the rebels to the brink, thus resulting in a record voter turnout.

However, as a result of a well-established political and military network, the Maoists still control half of at least four south Bastar districts and one-third of the rest. In Bijapur, most of the government-run welfare programmes are not allowed by the rebels; government officials never undertake any road construction projects without tacit approval from the local commanders; tribal constables request the Maoists to protect their families in at least one-third of the district.

➤ 5.10.4 Should Army be Deployed Against Naxals?

The army is trained to fight against an enemy country. Fighting with our own people is not the job of the army. In fact, the army is employed to protect its own people. It would be very difficult for the army to distinguish innocent people from hardcore Naxalites. The Army is a symbol of national pride. We must ensure that the image of the army is not affected. So, naxalism has to be fought by the police and other para military forces.

Also, a complete armed solution is not the only answer to naxalism. We should give more emphasis on effective administration, development and growth of the affected areas. As of now, it is not advisable to deploy Indian army against naxals. However, air support from army can be taken not for air strikes but for evacuation, supply, medical aid, etc.

PROBABLE QUESTIONS BASED ON THIS CHAPTER

1. Should army be deployed in left wing extremism affected areas? Justify your answer.
2. How much intellectual support to Naxalism is justified?
3. What are the basic features of Operation Greyhound?
4. What are the aims and objectives of Naxalites? Are they really the messiahs of downtrodden as they claim to be?
5. What are the factors responsible for the rise of Naxalism?

CHAPTER 6

Linkages Between Development and Spread of Extremism

UN Secretary General Kofi Annan once proclaimed, *'No one in this world can be comfortable or safe when so many people are suffering and deprived'*. Therefore, suffering and deprivation due to under-development are bound to have implications on issues of internal security.

Simply speaking, there are several areas in the country where crucial elements of survival, like food, shelter and clothing, are a luxury for people and these areas also lack basic infrastructure like roads, drinking water and electricity. In such cases, there is economic insecurity leading to crime and other anti-social activities.

6.1 Major Components of Development

Major components of development are:

1. *Economic development:* Employment, per capita income, industrial development
2. *Social development*: Gender equality, women empowerment, pluralism, respect for diversity, education of children, social security, etc.

3. *Political development*: Democracy, political rights, civil liberties
4. *Human development*: Health, education, human rights, life with dignity and self-esteem
5. *Infrastructure development*: Transport, communication, highways, rail network, telephone connectivity, cyber broadband network
6. *Sustainable development*: Ecological safety, environmental protection, biodiversity preservation
7. *Administrative development*: Good governance, time bound delivery of public services, public participation in government, transparency, accountability, pro-people governance

6.2 Factors Responsible for Spread of Extremism

The factors responsible for the spread of extremism are:

1. **Jal-Jangal-Jameen:** Disruption of age-old tribal–forest relationship, violation of traditional land rights, land acquisition without appropriate compensation and rehabilitation
2. **Economic:** Unemployment, poverty, infrastructure deficit like poor transport, lack of health facility, lack of education, communication and electricity, rising gap between rich and poor
3. **Social:** Social inequality, discrimination, denial of human rights, abuse of dignity of life
4. **Political:** Lack of people's participation in government
5. **Governance deficit:** Lack of routine administration, complete absence of government machinery in remote areas, poor implementation of laws, mismanagement and corruption in government schemes
6. **Ethnic**
7. **Geographical**
8. **Historical**

The first three factors are development deficit related factors that directly cause extremism. The fourth and fifth factors are not the root causes but give impetus to the already existing extremist feelings and are thus used by extremists to propagate their nefarious designs. The sixth, seventh and eighth are not related to development at all and they have their roots in history, geography and ethnicity and have been explained in detail in earlier chapters.

6.2.1 Development-linked Factors Applicable to India for Spread of Extremism

For growth of terrorism in a particular area, we need to have some fertile breeding ground. Poverty, unemployment and lack of development provide that fertile ground. Terrorism needs an ideology which could be in the name of religion, race and region or the Marxist ideology of egalitarian society. Combined with fertile ground and ideologies, lack of administration resulting in governance deficit along with political factors is used by hardcore ideologues to brainwash and radicalize the youth. Therefore, lack of development has direct as well as indirect linkages with extremism.

1. Jal-Jangal-Jameen Issues (Disruption of Age-old Relationship)

For centuries, tribals have a natural co-existential relationship with their natural habitat, i.e. forests. But modern legislations and governance in the last century considerably altered this age-old relationship. The Forest Act, 1927 and the Forest Conservation Act, 1980 along with stringent Supreme Court orders and developmental activities like mining, power projects and industrialization have taken away sources of their basic livelihood. The most important being the Forest Conservation Act, 1980. As per the Act, their traditional rights have been curtailed and they can no longer make a livelihood out of their habitat (forests). As a result, their old livelihood has been taken away and has not been replaced by the fruits of new development. They have access to neither the basic infrastructure (transport, communication and electricity), nor the consequent economic development which could provide them employment and rid them of poverty. This has resulted in a feeling of despair and deprivation among the tribals. Therefore, they are vulnerable to recruitment by extremist ideologues. They should have been given fair share in profit and royalty of mining and industries.

The tribal population has thus been fertile ground for recruitment for the left wing extremists. Coupled with poor governance and other social and political factors they have easily been converted into hardcore followers of the naxalite movement.

2. Economic Issues

Poverty, unemployment and lack of education continue to be portrayed as fundamental drivers of extremism. Poverty and unemployment are often blamed for creating feelings of hopelessness and desperation. Poor economic conditions foster lack of opportunities, resulting in a limited number of options for gainful employment. The unemployment pushes the youth towards the lure of extremist ideas. It is not surprising that the hotbeds of terrorism today– Afghanistan, Yemen, Somalia, Pakistan, Indonesia – happen to be some of the poorest and most corrupt countries in the world. Poverty and unemployment resulting in anger, resentment, despair and sense of injustice are a volatile combination in the minds of young men and women. These young minds can be manipulated to pick up arms. Individuals from higher income groups of society are more likely to have a range of economic activities available to them and are less likely to engage in terrorist activities. High levels of unemployment and higher gap between rich and poor also increases the potential for terror organizations to recruit educated, unemployed youth who are capable of carrying out more effective and brutal attacks.

3. Social Issues

High levels of social fragmentation, perception of exclusion and marginalization in some segments of society act as push factors for extremism. Relative deprivation and frustrated expectations for economic improvement and social mobility are also major drivers of extremism.

4. Political Issues

Political factors are also an indirect cause for spread of extremism. In places where human rights and democratic values are lacking, disaffected groups are more likely to opt for a path of violence. Extremism also flourishes due to severe restrictions on civil liberties and political rights. Civil liberties include freedom of expression, association, movement, and the press; freedom of, and from, religion; the right to due process; protection for individuals against unwarranted use of state power; and protection for minorities against potential encroachment on their fundamental rights that may result from majority rule. Political rights refer to the existence of rules and mechanisms (e.g., free and fair elections) that enable individuals and communities to affect governmental decision-making, and to participate in political processes more generally. These political factors are used by terrorist groups to brainwash educated unemployed youths to their ideology.

5. Governance Deficit

Ungoverned or poorly governed places may enable extremists to establish sanctuaries or safe havens. Poorly governed places may also create passive or active support for extremists among communities that feel ignored by the government. Where no government agency is able to provide for security and the rule of law, extremists may be able to impose their own order, and they may be able to extract money or recruits from the population.

Regarding the link between extremism and governance, stable democracy manages conflicts effectively by being open to political feedback about what is not working in the country, and by responding with remedial measures. But unfortunately, in India, over the years, the government has not been proactive in this regard. It ignored the legitimate grievances of the tribals of the North-east and Dandakaranya region. A society that does not respect principles of good governance, that is not transparent or accountable, and that does not respect the rule of law, finds it difficult to achieve sustainable development. Because the link between good governance and conflict is apparent, development is also tied to conflict and terrorism. Good governance is necessary to achieve sustainable development and to avoid, or at least manage, conflicts including terrorism.

6. Tri-junction Theory

According to this theory, areas situated around the tri-junction of borders of three states have the problem of governance-deficit. These areas lack transport, communication and other infrastructure. Dandakaranya – the worst affected Maoist area in the country is a perfect example of tri-junction theory.

Conclusion Terrorism has to have some basis, some ideology or some utopian goal so that a romantic illusion can be created in the minds of some sections of people, especially the younger generation. Sometimes, they use genuine issues like poverty, unemployment, etc. as a tool to attract masses to their cause. Many well meaning, liberal intellectuals fall prey to their propaganda without understanding the true nature of their doctrine which glorifies violence and believes in annihilation of all the people who are not with them. Sometimes, they create false issues by which their support base can be consolidated. But the underlying factor which fuels these movements is the visible lack of economic and social development. This is the basis of the insurgency movements in the North-east or Left Wing extremism in the country.

However the link between extremism and underdevelopment is not universal. J&K is an example where extremism is not because of underdevelopment but is due to historical and geographical reasons.

6.3 Positive Impact of Socio-Economic Development on Reducing Extremism

Social and economical development policies can contribute to peace and stability. The sections of society benefitted with development may start working to inhibit local support to extremists. It can discourage terrorist recruits. Many terrorist organizations attract new members from communities in which terrorism is generally considered a viable response to perceived grievances. Some terrorist groups also offer recruits financial incentives and additional family support. Social and economic development policies can help to reduce the pools of potential recruits by reducing their perceived grievances and providing the members of these communities with viable alternatives to terrorism. The ability of development policies to curb terrorism depends on their implementation. The most successful social and economic development policies are those that are

1. Developed in consultation with community leaders
2. Are based on needs and assessments that address the specific requirements of targeted communities, and
3. Are accompanied by disbursement mechanisms that ensure proper fiscal management and non-partisanship

Social and economic development policies can be used as a 'stick' to discourage terrorism. Development assistance can be made conditional on the absence of violence, thus discouraging support for terrorists.

We have successful examples of Tripura, Mizoram and other parts of the North-east where the spread of extremism ideology has been contained after robust and holistic development of these areas.

6.4 | Constitutional and Legal Safeguards for Tribal Population

1. The **Fifth Schedule** states briefly that all scheduled areas of the country which are forest reserves and inhabited by scheduled tribes are to be administered by the governors of the states by appointing tribal advisory councils from among the tribal community of a particular forest reserve or a scheduled area. Regrettably, this has not happened in India. In this vacuum, these forests have been leased for mining, thereby displacing the tribal communities.

2. The **Ninth Schedule** of the Constitution deals with the fact that cultivable land which over thousands of years had come under the ownership of upper castes should be acquired by the government and redistributed among India's landless peasantry. Since land revenue was a state subject, the states were to legislate land ceiling laws and implement them by acquiring farmlands from landlords and redistributing them to landless farmers who for centuries worked on the lands of the landowners. Regrettably, only three states, Jammu and Kashmir, West Bengal and Kerala, had implemented the land ceiling laws legislated by all the states by 1955. In West Bengal, the jotedars—as the landlords are called there—tried to manipulate the land records and deceive landless farmers and the government. This resulted in an uprising in a village called Naxalbari led by the Communist Party of India, Marxist-Leninist (CPI-ML), a faction of the Communist party. In Kerala, land ceiling was successfully implemented in the non-hilly districts and this has prevented the Maoist Naxalites from organizing a revolution there.

3. Politically, the **PESA, (Panchayats Extension to Scheduled Areas) Act, 1996** gives radical governance powers to the tribal community and recognizes its traditional community rights over local natural resources. It not only accepts the validity of 'customary law, social and religious practices, and traditional management practices of community resources', but also directs the state governments not to make any law which is inconsistent with these. Accepting a clear-cut role for the community, it gives wide-ranging powers to Gram Sabhas, which had hitherto been denied to them by the lawmakers of the country.

The ground reality, however, is still quite different and PESA has mostly been reduced to a paper tiger. The two fundamental responsible factors are the mindset of the government functionaries who are contemptuous of the tribal community and the existing state government laws and provisions that negate the PESA Act.

PESA Act is for rural areas, but a similar legislation for urban scheduled areas was never debated and enacted. State governments are taking advantage of this to give speedy clearances to mining and industries in tribal areas. Their modus operandi is simple: they upgrade rural panchayats in scheduled areas to urban panchayats to bypass PESA which mandates village council's approval for such projects.

In the past few years, more than 600 village panchayats, many of them in scheduled areas, have been converted into urban local bodies, and these areas have major industrial investment proposals.

4. **Forests Rights Act 2006** recognizes and vests the forest rights of occupation to the Scheduled Tribes and other traditional forest dwellers who have been residing in such forests for generations but whose rights could not be recorded. The Act is an important instrument for improving the livelihoods of people dependant on forests by securing land rights. Before this Act came into force, there were nearly forty lakh tribal people not possessing legal status to their lands.

Some of the major concerns regarding implementation of this Act are related to high rate of rejection of claims, very little progress in the recognition of community rights and habitat rights of Particularly Vulnerable Tribal Groups (PVTGs), convening of Gram Sabha meetings at the Panchayat level, insistence of particular form of evidence, claimants not being informed about rejection of claims and inadequate awareness.

5. **Prevention of Atrocities on SC/ST Act 1989** was brought into force with effect from 30th January, 1990 with the main objective 'to prevent the commission of offences of atrocities against members of the Scheduled Castes and the Scheduled Tribes, to provide for Special Courts for the trial of such offences and for the relief and rehabilitation of the victims of such offences and for matters connected therewith or incidental thereto'.

6. **New Land Acquisition Act (The Right to Fair Compensation and Transparency in Land Acquisition, Rehabilitation and Resettlement Act, 2013)** regulates land acquisition and provides laid down rules for granting compensation, rehabilitation and resettlement to the affected persons in India. The Act has provisions to provide fair compensation to those whose land is taken away, bring transparency to the process of acquisition of land to set up factories or buildings, infrastructural projects and assured rehabilitation of those affected. The Act establishes regulations for land acquisition as a part of India's massive industrialization drive driven by public-private partnership.

6.5 What Should be Done?

Our mission should be to end left wing extremism by ending extreme poverty and rampant unemployment. Anger, resentment, and despair are a volatile combination in the minds of young men and women who see little hope for escaping their situation. The goal of development is to eradicate poverty, promote inclusion and social justice, to bring the marginalized into the economic and global mainstream. Building of capacity is the essence of development and is a long-term process. The following are some of the steps required:

1. Sensitization to local context and customs, and addressing the critical needs of conflict-affected communities
2. Giving more emphasis to topics like community development, governance, service delivery, human rights, and political grievances
3. Effective implementation of protective legislation

4. Intense dialogue, so as to arrive at conclusions
5. Improved infrastructure and large investment in infrastructure
6. Protecting tribal rights
7. Employment opportunities through tax holidays to investments in those areas
8. Ensuring social security, livelihood security
9. Food security and education
10. Land reforms and equitable distribution of infrastructure projects
11. Constructive dialogue with extremists
12. Prosperity for all people
13. Anti-corruption efforts
14. End of political marginalization, social discrimination, cultural humiliation, violence by state functionaries, human rights abuses, and social oppression
16. Ensuring minimum wages and proper implementation of labour laws

Probable Questions Based on this Chapter

1. What are the linkages between development and the spread of left wing extremism? Explain with suitable examples.
2. Is underdevelopment the sole reason for the rise of extremism?

CHAPTER 7

Communal Violence

7.1 Secularism—Indian Context

India is a multi-religious, multi-ethnic and multi-cultural pluralist society. Unity in such diversity is the uniqueness of the Indian society. The Indian Constitution is a precious document of lasting value that preserves the composite culture and promotes the essence of Indian polity. The Constitution through its Preamble, Fundamental Rights and Directive Principles has created a secular state based on the principle of equality and non-discrimination. The Supreme Court has included 'secularism' in its doctrine of Basic Structure which cannot be amended even by Parliament.

The Indian model of secularism means equal treatment and equal respect for all religions by the State to endorse communal harmony and religious tolerance. It is basically derived from the doctrines of '*Sarva Dharm Sambhav*' and '*Sarva Dharm Sadbhav*'. Unlike the western model of secularism which envisions complete separation of religion and state, the Indian model is based on non-discrimination and equal participation by the State in all religions.

7.2 Historical Background

The seeds of the present communal violence were sown in the aftermath of the freedom struggle and Partition. The partition of Bengal on communal lines by Lord Curzon in 1905 can be considered as an attempt by the British to communalise Indian society and the political structure. The formation of Muslim League in 1906, and the introduction of separate electorates on communal lines in 1909 through the Morley-Minto reforms and the creation of Hindu Mahasabha in 1915 is believed to be the beginning of modern day communalism in India. The two-nation theory adopted by the Muslim League led to the division of this country into two separate sovereign nations. Partition resulted in displacement of nearly 14 million people with estimated loss of life of 2-3 million people. The violent nature of the partition created an atmosphere of mutual hostility and suspicion between Hindus and Muslims.

After partition, India has seen recurrent communal riots in different parts of the country. A rise in fundamentalist feelings occurred due to the Shah Bano case in 1986 and Ayodhya events of 1990s. On one hand, there was a growing feeling of fear among Muslims. On the other hand, Hindus opposed the so called pseudo-secularists and appeasement policies of successive governments. After 1992, post Ayodhya riots spread almost all over the country. Mumbai even witnessed bomb blasts. Again the Godhra and post Godhra riots of 2002 further disturbed communal harmony in the country. In 2013, communal clashes in Muzaffarnagar and adjoining districts of western Uttar Pradesh have further vitiated the atmosphere. The Ministry of Home Affairs' data on communal violence nationwide reveals that there has been a decline in communal incidents from 2008 till 2011 but a sharp increase was recorded in 2012 and 2013. The year 2013 saw more deaths due to communal riots than the entire three-year period of 2010–2012. Uttar Pradesh accounted for 35 percent of the communal incidents across the country in 2013.

Recent years have seen a growth of both Muslim and Hindu chauvinistic organizations. Though Indian Muslims have, by and large, resisted continuous efforts at radicalization, but due to political and criminal exploitation of communal sentiments, fringe elements within the Muslim community remain vulnerable to mobilization, recruitment and radicalization by hostile anti-India forces that have always been looking to wage a proxy sub-conventional war against India.

7.3 Factors Responsible for Communal Riots

The following factors are responsible for communal riots.

1. **Historical factors:** The history of Partition and the two-nation theory have generated a deep sense of communalism and lack of mutual trust among both the communities. It discouraged a harmonious association and peaceful co-existence.
2. **Political factors:** Divide and rule policy practised by the British and the subsequent vote-bank politics followed by Indian political parties after Independence have added to the divide between the communities. Lack of liberal, progressive and modern attitude in both communities has also weakened the cause of communal harmony.

3. **Educational factors:** There is lack of modern education among a large section of Indian society. A majority of Indians failed to adopt a scientific and technological approach, hence are reluctant to adopt liberal, progressive values.
4. **Socio-economic factors:** Due to their educational backwardness, the Muslims have not been represented sufficiently in public services, industry and trade, etc. Their economic status is very low. This causes the feeling of relative deprivation and such feelings contain the seeds of communalism.
5. **Psychological factors:** Psychological factors play an important role in the development of communalism. Both communities have perceived grudges against each other. There is a sort of fear psychosis amongst Muslims. These lead to communal ill-feelings.
6. **Identity crisis or identity factors:** There is a feeling that Muslims are reluctant to join the national mainstream. Most of them do not enthusiastically participate in secular nationalistic politics and insist on maintaining their separate identity.
7. **Cultural factors:** Orthodox members of both communities feel that they have a distinct entity with their own cultural pattern, personal laws and thought processes. There are strong elements of conservatism and fundamentalism among both the communities.
8. **The ISI factor:** It is widely believed that the ISI is directly encouraging and promoting communalism by instigating hard core fundamentalist elements of Indian Muslim community. It is also believed that vulnerable youth are trained by ISI to destabilize India's internal security by spreading communal venom.
9. **Influence of international Pan-Islamic Jehadi movements:** Pan-Islamic movements have also been mobilizing anti-India Jehadi sentiments in the context of the Kashmir issue and the Gujarat riots.
10. **Demographic factors:** Demographic changes in Assam, West Bengal and the Kashmir Valley create opportunities for manipulation of communal sentiments for short-term political objectives.
11. **Social media factors:** Negative impact of social media in spreading rumours, disinformation, hate-campaign and fanning violence.
12. **Organized criminal involvement:** Underworld criminals like Dawood Ibrahim, Chhota Shakeel, etc. are believed to have a key role in acting as agents of vested interest in instigating communal riots. There is also lack of political and social consciousness towards building a harmonious, coexistent society. We also need to build a nationalistic consciousness where the nation is above everything else.
13. **Lack of strong action:** Lack of strong and decisive action by police and allegations of biased or delayed action by them are also a cause. Real perpetrators are rarely punished and there is lack of fear of law that could prevent them from instigating communal riots.

7.3.1 Immediate Flash Points for Riots

There are many causes why communal riots flare up:

1. *Gender offences*: Offences like eve teasing, molestation, rape, elopement with girls/boys of other community. Hindu organizations attribute such elopement and marriages as part of a conspiracy, namely 'love jehad'.
2. *Land disputes:* Disputes over ownership of land belonging to graveyards, construction on new place of worship, unauthorized construction, claims and counter claims over old constructions at places of worship as well as demolition.
3. *Religious festivities*: During celebration of Holi, Eid, Moharram, etc. many local disputes arise between the two communities which have a potential to flare up.

7.4 The Way Forward

The following measures need to be implemented to curb the menace of communal violence:

1. **Taking pride in our heritage:** The feelings of nationalism should be inculcated in the minds of people by reminding them about the glorious moments of freedom struggle wherein Hindus, Muslims and Sikhs were united in the fight against the British to safeguard the interests of the country.
2. **Impartial administration and police:** Most riots persist for longer periods because people feel that the administration/police is not impartial. Changing this perception is most crucial for stopping riots. Perceived political interference in administration during communal violence must be eliminated. The directives of police reforms given by the Hon. Supreme Court should be adopted by state Governments in letter and spirit. A fixed tenure of District Magistrate/Deputy Commissioner and Superintendent of Police, SHO and Field officers will make a big difference.
3. **Policy of zero-tolerance towards violence:** Government policy and practices should be firm and strict in this regard. It should not be affected by vote-bank politics. Police must take immediate, strong and effective action against those who indulge in violence irrespective of their community. There is an urgent need of not just an effective civil administration but also a speedy judiciary. Strict bail provisions must be made in cases of communal violence on the lines of the NDPS Act.
4. **Peace committees:** Peace committees should be mandatory in every area. It should include secular and visionary people from all communities. People with high social standing like doctors, philanthropists and social workers must be engaged with such peace committees. Meetings of peace committee should be organized regularly. The district administration should engage actively with such committees to promote communal harmony.

5. **Win people's hearts through media and civil society:** The faith of common people in the local police should be restored with the help of civil society, NGOs and media. Community policing and beat-constable system is also helpful in gathering intelligence and grass-roots information.
6. **Sensitise police towards feelings of minorities:** The minority community at large views the police as communal and biased against them. Police must be sensitised to feelings of minorities and build trust.
7. **Holistic development of minority communities:** There should be a sincere effort to ensure that employment and skill development opportunities are available in the economic, educational and social spheres for the minority communities. Efforts should be made for bringing them in the mainstream of Indian society.
8. **Impart liberal values:** Government should impart liberal values in our society through our education system. Soft skill development training should be provide to police and administration personnel.
9. **Strong legal action:** The police should take adequate steps to identify in advance potential trouble makers and make timely use of preventive sections of law. Those inciting communal feelings must be punished. Provocative speeches by religious leaders in public and media must be dealt with strictly and strong legal action should be taken against them.
10. **Positive utilization of social media and mass media for awareness:** The misuse of social media and mass media should be prevented. Efforts should be made through mass media for changing the attitude of people towards other communities. People must be made aware of the evils of communalism. Government should sponsor movies promoting communal harmony and secularism.
11. **Proper checks and balances on social media:** Rumours/hate propaganda can be prevented through control of bulk SMSes in times of communal tension.
12. Need to evolve early warning signals to prevent communal flare ups.
13. **Ban on contesting elections:** People charge sheeted in cases of communal violence should be banned from contesting elections.
14. Special fast track courts to deal with communal riot cases and bail norms must be strict.
15. **Manpower shortage issue in police:** The number of policemen per one lakh people in India is only 130. The minimum United Nations norm is 220. This gap should be filled.
16. A fair representation of marginalized section of society in police and other security forces.
17. Capacity building of police and implementation of police reforms.
18. Identification of miscreants and action against provocateurs.
19. Videography of riots and strict legal action against rioters.
20. Creation of sources in communally sensitive areas.
21. Preventing community based ghettos in urban areas.
22. Formulating counter-radicalization and de-radicalization policies.

PROBABLE QUESTIONS BASED ON THIS CHAPTER

1. What are the fundamental reasons for the rise of communal feelings in a society? Explain this with suitable examples in the context of India.
2. Is communalism the biggest threat to the country's unity? Explain with relevant examples.
3. What measures would you suggest for curbing communal violence and establishing a progressive, liberal and peaceful society in India?

CHAPTER 8

Organised Crime

8.1 What is the Meaning of the Term 'Organised Crime'?

Organised crime means '*a structured group of three or more persons existing for a period of time and acting in concert with the aim of committing serious crimes or offences to obtain, directly or indirectly, financial or other material benefit*'.

It manifests in many forms. Organised crime can be further classified into two categories, *viz*, traditional organised crime and non-traditional (modern) organised crime.

Traditional organised crime includes illicit liquor trade, betting, gambling, kidnapping, extortion, prostitution rackets, robbery, blackmailing, sand mafia, mining mafia, contract killing, pornography, etc.

Non-traditional organised crime includes transnational crime like money laundering, pumping fake Indian currency notes (FICN), *hawala* transfer, cybercrime, hacking, human trafficking, arms smuggling, drugs smuggling, etc.

8.2 What is Transnational Organised Crime?

As per UN Convention, transnational organised crime comprises

- A group of three or more persons that was not randomly formed;
- Existence of such a group for a period of time;

- Acting in concert with the aim of committing at least one crime punishable by at least four years' incarceration;
- In order to obtain, directly or indirectly, a financial or other material benefit.

Since most 'groups' of any sort contain three or more people working in concert and most exist for a period of time, the true defining characteristics of organised crime groups under the UN Convention are their profit-driven nature and the seriousness of the offences they commit. The following table defines organised crime and terrorism and compares traditional versus modern versions.

	Traditional	Modern
Organised Crime	Based on power over local communities	Based on expansion of global markets
	Family organisation	Networks of entrepreneurs
Terrorism	Based on support in oppressed communities	Based on sympathisers in several countries
	Military model of top-to-bottom organisation	Networks of ideologically committed operatives

➤ 8.2.1 Link Between Organised Crime and Terrorism

Terrorists engage in organised crime to support themselves financially. Drugs trafficking, money laundering, FICN, supari killing and extortion are the main organised crimes by which terrorists generate money.

Organised crime groups and terrorists often operate on same network structures. Terrorists thrive under the cloak of transnational organised crime groups. Both organised crime groups and terrorist groups operate in areas with little governmental controls, weak enforcement of laws and open borders. Both often use similar means of modern technology to communicate.

These groups may provide smuggled arms and explosives to terrorist groups in exchange for drugs or diamonds, etc. Terrorist groups make use of smuggling networks established by organised crime to move operatives around the world. Criminal groups also provide money laundering services. Terrorist groups controlling the terrain tax drug traffickers in return for protection.

Organised crime and terrorism thrive on ineffective governance, poor checks and balances. They have developed a symbiotic relationship. But neither are all terrorist acts organised crime, nor are all organised criminal acts terrorism; in most developed countries, organised crime thrives with little or no terrorist activities, and in most developing countries, terrorism exists along with varying levels of organised criminal activity.

➤ 8.2.2 Major Differences Between Organised Crime and Terrorism

The differences between them rest on means and ends. Terrorism aims to overthrow the existing government by altering the status quo. Organised crime, on the other hand, aims to form a parallel government(parallel economy) while co-existing with the existing one; any change in the status quo is only circumstantial or a by-product and born out of convenience rather than zealous revisionist policy. Secondly, terrorism primarily uses violent means, whereas organised crime prefers to be non-violent notwithstanding the odd resort to belligerence. Third, terrorism is driven purely by political objectives despite sometimes resorting to exploitation of regional, national and religious sentiments to achieve their ends; conversely, economic objectives are the operational determinants of organised crime.

8.3 Different Types of Organised Crime

Different types of organised crime include:

- Narcotics trafficking
- Arms trafficking
- Human smuggling
- Gold smuggling
- Fake currency
- Kidnapping and extortion
- Contract killing/supari killing
- Cyber crime
- Money laundering
- Maritime piracy
- CBRN smuggling (Chemical, Biological, Radiological and Nuclear Defence)
- Trading in human body parts
- Infiltration of illegal businesses

It is worth mentioning that the first five activities in the above list are more prone to have terrorist linkages.

8.4 What are the Links Between Terrorism and Organised Crime and How are They Relevant in the Indian Context?

More than ever before, groups engaged in terrorism and organised crime operate together. These relationships have helped terrorist groups to be less dependent on state sponsors, and on their domestic and international supporters. The 1990s, especially the second half, witnessed a number of terrorist groups learning from criminal networks. Operating through the cover of sympathetic organisations in Europe and North America, many Asia-Pacific terrorist groups generate huge revenues from video and CD piracy, business in phone cards and credit card scams.

While organised crime involves many activities, its linkages with terrorism stem from illegal trafficking of drugs, arms and human beings, fake currency and money laundering. Terrorist groups, whether indigenous or sponsored by outside states, need arms and money for their fight against the security forces. Organised crime needs a client and couriers who can smuggle drugs, arms and human beings across countries and regions.

In India, the linkages between the two exist at national and transnational levels. At the national level, both terrorists and those involved in organised crime are within India. At the international level, collaboration exists between transnational syndicates and terrorists from inside and outside India.

➤ 8.4.1 Links Between Terrorism and Organised Crime in the North-East

In India's north-east, almost all militant groups run a parallel government or have their areas of influence and are involved in collecting money directly from the people. Much of the government funds reach the militants indirectly due to mal-governance. Government officials in conflict zones are either threatened or bribed to award contracts to individuals patronised by the militant groups. Contracts apart, essential commodities like rice and fuel reach the militant groups directly which are then sold to the public at much higher prices. This phenomenon, though unnoticed in other parts of India, is a clear example of the linkage between organised crime and terrorism inside India.

Extortion, kidnapping, contracts and black marketing still fall short of financing the nefarious activities of the militants. This is where transnational drugs and arms syndicates come into play. Terrorist organisations, especially in the north-east, mobilise funds by becoming couriers of illegal drugs and arms, and at times even human beings, from one point to another within the country. Some of the infamous entry points from South-east Asia include Moreh and the entire Chittagong Hill tracts, especially Cox's Bazaar. Initially, international criminal syndicates had their own network; however, with these routes being taken over by various terrorist groups in the north-eastern states, the syndicates have started using them instead of bribing them to let their consignments get through.

➤ 8.4.2 Links Between Terrorism and Organised Crime in Kashmir

In Kashmir, the linkages between terrorists and organised crime exist at a different level. Unlike the north-east, reliance on funds from extortion and other related means is minimal. There is no parallel government in Kashmir and government resources do not reach militant hands. However, external funds compensate for inadequate internal mobilisation. External funds reach the militant organisations fighting in Kashmir through various means. For instance, enormous funds mobilised in Pakistan and other Muslim countries, especially in the Gulf, are channelled through various organisations in Pakistan to Kashmir. Markazdawa al Arshad, for example, mobilises funds from inside and outside Pakistan to support its militant wing, Lashkar-e-Toiba. Besides, external funds are also routed through select organisations and individuals in Kashmir, which finally reach the militants. Money laundering plays a significant role. Hawala transactions take place swiftly and effectively. Besides, it is also believed that the ISI uses drug money to fund militant activities in the state.

Another significant relationship between organised crime and terrorism, especially in Kashmir, is through the spread of counterfeit currency, FICN. Terrorists are the main couriers of Indian counterfeit currency inside Kashmir, which then spreads all over India. Even guides for the militants from across the border are paid with counterfeit money. In fact, when some of the 'indigenous' militants were also paid with counterfeits, it resulted in squabble between them and the so-called guest militants.

➤ 8.4.3 Links Between Terrorism and Organised Crime in the Rest of India

Besides Kashmir and the north-east, sporadic incidents in other parts of India, like the Mumbai blasts, for instance, have exposed the connection between terrorism and organised crime. This is distinct from the traditional linkages flourishing between organised crime syndicates and local criminals.

Bombay Blast

Bomabay Blast 1993 was a classical example of organized crime cartel's planning and executing terrorist activities. The 1993 Bombay bombings were a series of 13 bomb explosions that took place in Bombay on Friday, 12 March 1993. The coordinated attacks were the most destructive bomb explosions in Indian history. The single-day attacks resulted in over 350 fatalities and 1200 injuries.

The attacks were coordinated by Dawood Ibrahim, don of the Bombay-based international organised crime syndicate named D-Company. Dawood Ibrahim was the mastermind behind these blasts. He is involved in all kind of organized crime cartels like Drugs smuggling, gold smuggling, Supari killing, match-fixing etc.

Linkages between terrorism and organized crime came to limelight first time in India in Bombay blast. Communal tension led to terror activities first time in India. First time revenge of riots was taken in the form of terror attacks.

Dawood Ibrahim

Dawood Ibrahim is the most powerful Mumbai Mafia 'don', with a countrywide network and extensive linkages abroad. He is a classic example of Organized crime Mafia. He is one of the most powerful gangsters involved in transnational crimes, including narcotics smuggling, extortion and contract killing. It is believed that he lives in Pakistan and Dubai with support from ISI, though ISI denies it.

Dawood Ibrahim was believed to control much of the hawala system, which is the commonly used unofficial system for transferring money and remittances outside the view of official agencies. He is currently on the wanted list of Interpol for Cheating, Criminal Conspiracy and Organised Crime Syndicated. He was No. 3 on the Forbes' World's Top 10 most dreaded criminals list of 2011, rising from the 4th position in 2008.

According to the United States, Dawood Ibrahim maintained close links with Al-Qaeda's Osama Bin Laden. As a consequence, the United States declared Dawood Ibrahim a "global terrorist" in 2003 and pursued the matter before the United Nations in an attempt to freeze his assets around the world and crack down on his operations. The US administration imposed several sanctions on Ibrahim and his associates. Indian and Russian intelligence agencies have pointed out Ibrahim's possible involvement in several other terror attacks, including the November 2008 Mumbai attacks.

Currently, the primary activities of this gang are extortion, contract killing, film financing, match-fixing, drug trafficking, smuggling gold and computer parts and illicit trade in arms and ammunition. The Dawood gang has been supplying arms both to criminals and terrorists.

➤ 8.4.4 Links Between Terrorism and Money Laundering

Terrorist groups have begun to lay a premium on gaining domestic respectability, as also international acceptance, for their goals. Accordingly, such groups have gradually tended to distance themselves from visibly illegitimate businesses and to invest in legitimate businesses like investment in share market, capital market, IPL spot-fixing, etc. Specifically, with regard to organised crime, terrorist groups have taken advantage of existing laws to further their own agenda of establishing a transnational network. Irrespective of who does it, it is not a criminal offence in most countries to generate funds through businesses and raise funds through charities. A large proportion of 'dirty money' can be traced to proliferating narcotics cartels, alien smuggling networks, etc. But law enforcement agencies find it more difficult to detect *clean-clean* money (money which is both generated and transferred legally) as compared to *dirty-clean* money (money generated from criminal operations and 'laundered'). The former has certain legitimacy and no illegal hooks attached. With governments allocating significant resources to combat money laundering, it is becoming difficult for terrorist groups to rely on criminal proceeds. The latest United Nations (UN) Conventions on (a) the Suppression of the Financing of Terrorism and (b) Transnational Organised Crime will make money laundering even harder.

In order to evade the police dragnet, terrorist groups are consequently developing and maintaining clean money sources. Accordingly, the future scenario is likely to see rag-tag/groups-in-transition utilising 'dirty-clean money routes' and sophisticated groups using 'clean-clean money routes'. Emerging trends in organised crime indicate that most groups with a national reach are involved in illegitimate businesses, e.g., narcotics and alien smuggling, abduction, extortion, etc. At the other end, a majority of the groups with a global reach are involved in legitimate/quasi-legitimate businesses, e.g., manufacturing, CD/video piracy, etc.

➤ 8.4.5 Links Between Terrorism and Drug Trafficking

Heroin from the Golden Crescent (Afghanistan, Iran and Pakistan) and Golden Triangle (Myanmar, Laos and Thailand) feeds the Asia-Pacific – a region with major transit routes to Europe and North America.

The increase in consumption within the region has also contributed to regional insecurity because of the terrorist-criminal nexus. While organised crime groups that are often linked to terrorist groups control narcotics distribution, many terrorist and guerrilla groups control the territories where the narcotics are cultivated or refined. The erstwhile Taliban regime controlled parts of Afghanistan where heroin was produced and taxed the cultivators as also the transporters of opium. Furthermore, the threat posed by narcotics to health, economic, and law and order spheres in the region is on the increase.

Narcotic trafficking is a major source of revenue for terrorists and organised crime networks, particularly groups with trans-state reach. As much as armed ethnic groups in Myanmar control the flow of narcotics from Myanmar, armed Islamic groups tax and control organised crime networks regulating the flow of narcotics from Afghanistan. Organised crime, already prevalent in the Far East and South-east Asia, has gained a prominent foothold in the cities of South Asia since the mid-1990s. Organised crime networks in Japan, Hong Kong and China have also made greater inroads in the West. With South Asia increasingly moving towards a market economy, it is likely that organised crime will take deeper roots.

➤ 8.5 The Future of the Links Between Terrorism and Organised Crime and How They Can be Broken

With the loss of state sponsorship for terrorism, terrorist groups need to pursue different means of financing, mainly through arms and drugs trafficking. Terrorist dependence on organised crime for financial viability and organisational survival will increase in the near future. Structurally, terrorist groups will increasingly mirror organised crime groups. Terrorist groups will rapidly move in search of new opportunities to generate funds. Dependent on the financial opportunities available, both sources and methods of generating revenue will differ from one another. With state-sponsors distancing themselves, terrorist groups will either develop robust organised crime components or work closely with organised crime groups. While the bulk of the terrorist groups will retain their political leanings, the potential for a few terrorist groups to degenerate into pure criminal groups will, nevertheless, increase.

To effectively combat international terrorism, state response will have to factor in the nexus between terrorists and organised crime.

Among the principal responses to regulating these existing and emerging threats are:

- Develop exceptionally good military and intelligence expertise to neutralise terrorist groups. The approach of punishing individuals, but permitting groups that have perpetrated violence to exist, is highly counterproductive.
- Develop arrangements with states to disrupt terrorist support networks and assist states by sharing intelligence and exchanging personnel to fight transnational terrorist networks.
- Terrorist groups can be effectively crushed only at an early stage. The failure to fight efficiently, legitimately and ethically — especially against an ethnically and religiously empowered group — can lead to indiscriminate violence, which can favour the terrorists. With time, most conflicts can gather momentum generating substantial popular support. In such instances, a political solution over a military solution should be considered.
- Often, devolving regional autonomy or power sharing has been the most effective strategy. But, it works primarily in the formative phases of a conflict. The process requires close supervision, particularly during the implementation phase.
- A politico-military approach should be evolved to politically isolate a group in order to stem support and recruits, and to simultaneously offer political and economic incentives and to militarily pressurise it to join the mainstream. Often, links with foreign groups, state sponsors, or diaspora-support can provide the confidence to fight on. Transnational networks make such groups more resilient.
- Stringent law like TADA, MCOCA, Gangster Act, etc. to deal with organised crime
- While some of these threats can be resolved unilaterally by states, most require bilateral and multilateral arrangements.
- Some of the threats can be regulated at the sub-regional and others at the regional level.
- Some of the threats are new, others are old, but have assumed a renewed dimension. Therefore, new institutions capable of delivering multi-pronged responses are essential to regulate extant and emerging threats.

8.6 UN Convention against Transnational Organised Crime and the Protocols

UNTOC is the guardian of the United Nations Convention against Transnational Organised Crime(Organised Crime Convention) and the three Protocols (Trafficking in Persons, Smuggling of Migrants and Trafficking of Firearms) that supplement it.

This is the only international convention, which deals with organised crime. It is a landmark achievement, representing the international community's commitment to combating transnational organised crime and acknowledging the UN's role in supporting this commitment. The adoption of the Convention at the fifty-fifth session of the General Assembly of the United Nations in 2000 and its entry into force in 2003 also marked a historic commitment by the international community to counter organised crime.

The Organised Crime Convention offers states which are party to the convention, a framework for preventing and combating organised crime, and a platform for cooperating in doing so. These states have committed to establishing the criminal offences of participating in an organised crime group, money laundering, corruption and obstruction of justice in their national legislation. By becoming parties to the UNTOC, these states also have access to a new framework for mutual legal assistance and extradition, as well as a platform for strengthening law enforcement cooperation. States have also committed to promoting training and technical assistance to strengthen the capacity of national authorities to address organised crime.

8.7 Money Laundering

The process of creating the appearance that large amounts of money obtained from serious crimes, such as drug trafficking or terrorist activity, is from a legitimate source is called *money laundering*. The process of making 'dirty money' look like 'clean money' is referred to as money laundering.

Money laundering is a crucial step in the success of drug trafficking and terrorist activities. The connection between money laundering and terrorism may be a bit more complex, but it plays a crucial role in the sustainability of terrorist organisations. Most people who financially support terrorist organisations do not simply write a personal cheque and hand it over to a member of the terrorist group. They send the money in roundabout ways that allow them to fund terrorism while maintaining anonymity. On the other end, terrorists do not use credit cards and cheques to purchase the weapons, plane tickets and civilian assistance; they need to carry out a plot. They launder the money so that authorities cannot trace it back to them and foil their planned attack. Interrupting the laundering process can cut off funding and resources to terrorist groups.

The basic money laundering process has three steps:

- **Placement:** At this stage, the launderer inserts the dirty money into a legitimate financial institution. This is often in the form of cash bank deposits. This is the riskiest stage of the laundering process because large amounts of cash are pretty conspicuous, and banks are required to report high-value transactions.
- **Layering:** Layering involves sending the money through various financial transactions to change its form and make it difficult to follow. Layering may consist of several bank-to-bank transfers, wire transfers between different accounts in different names in different countries, making deposits and withdrawals to continually vary the amount of money in the accounts, changing the money's currency, and purchasing high-value

items (boats, houses, cars and diamonds) to change the form of the money. This is the most complex step in any laundering scheme, and it's all about making the original dirty money as hard to trace as possible.

- **Integration:** At the integration stage, the money re-enters the mainstream economy in a legitimate-looking form—it appears to come from a legal transaction. This may involve a final bank transfer into the account of a local business in which the launderer is 'investing' in exchange for a cut of the profits. At this point, the criminal can use the money without getting caught. It's very difficult to catch a launderer during the integration stage if there is no documentation during the previous stages.

➤ 8.7.1 The Effects of Money Laundering

Criminals launder anywhere between $500 billion and $1 trillion worldwide every year. The global effect is staggering in social, economic and security terms.

Social Effects

On the socio-cultural end of the spectrum, successfully laundering money means that criminal activity actually does pay off. This success encourages criminals to continue their illicit schemes because they get to spend the profit with no repercussions. This means more fraud, more corporate embezzling (which means more workers losing their pensions when the corporation collapses), more drugs on the streets, more drug-related crime, law-enforcement resources stretched beyond their means and a general loss of morale on the part of legitimate business people who donot break the law and donot make nearly the profits that the criminals do.

Economic Effects

The economic effects are on a broader scale. Developing countries often bear the brunt of modern money laundering because the governments are still in the process of establishing regulations for their newly privatised financial sectors. This makes them prime target. Other major issues facing the world's economies include errors in economic policy resulting from artificially inflated financial sectors. Massive influx of dirty cash into particular areas of the economy that are desirable to money launderers create false demand, and officials act on this new demand by adjusting economic policy. When the laundering processes reaches a certain point or if law-enforcement officials start to show interest, all that money suddenly disappears without any predictable economic cause and that financial sector falls apart.

Some problems on a more local scale relate to taxation and small-business competition. Laundered money is usually untaxed, meaning the rest of us ultimately have to make up the loss in tax revenue. Also, legitimate small businesses cannot compete with moneylaundering front businesses that can afford to sell a product far cheaper because their primary purpose is to get clean money, not earn profit. They have so much cash coming in that they might even sell a product or service below cost.

➤ 8.7.2 Trade-based Money Laundering (TBML)

Financial Action Task Force (FATF) defines **Trade Based Money Laundering (TBML)** as the process of disguising the proceeds of crime and moving value through the use of trade transactions in an attempt to legitimise their illicit origins. In simpler terms, TBML is the process of transferring/moving money through trade transactions. In practice, this can be achieved through the misrepresentation of the price, quantity or quality of imports or export.

The basic techniques of trade-based money laundering include:

1. **Over-invoicing and 'Under-invoicing' of goods and services:** Money laundering through the over-invoicing and under-invoicing of goods and services, which is one of the oldest methods of fraudulently transferring value across borders, remains a common practice today. The key element of this technique is the misrepresentation of the price of the good or service in order to transfer additional value between the importer and the exporter. Over-invoicing of exports is one of the most common trade-based money laundering techniques used to move money. This reflects the fact that the primary focus of most customs agencies is to stop the import of contraband and ensure that appropriate import duties are collected.
2. **Multiple-invoicing of goods and services:** Another technique used to launder funds involves issuing more than one invoice for the same trade transaction. By invoicing the same good or service more than once, a money launderer or terrorist financier is able to justify multiple payments for the same shipment of goods or delivery of services. Unlike over-invoicing and under-invoicing, it should be noted that there is no need for the exporter or importer to misrepresent the price of the good or service on the commercial invoice.
3. **Over-shipment and under-shipment of goods and services:** In addition to manipulating export and import prices, a money launderer can overstate or understate the quantity of goods being shipped or services being provided. In the extreme case, an exporter may not ship any goods at all, but simply collude with an importer to ensure that all shipping and customs documents associated with this so called 'phantom shipment' are routinely processed. Banks and other financial institutions may unknowingly be involved in the provision of trade financing for these phantom shipments.
4. **Falsely described goods and services:** In addition to manipulating export and import prices, a money launderer can misrepresent the quality or type of a good or service. For example, an exporter may ship a relatively inexpensive good and falsely invoice it as a more expensive item or an entirely different item. This creates a discrepancy between what appears on the shipping and customs documents and what is actually shipped. The use of false descriptions can also be used in the trade in services, such as financial advice, consulting services and market research. Generally, cases of over-invoicing or under-invoicing primarily designed to gain a tax advantage are considered customs fraud as also other manifestations as above.

➤ 8.7.3 Prevention of Money Laundering Act (PMLA)

PMLA is a criminal law which came into force on July 1, 2005. Under the Act, money laundering linked to the predicate scheduled offences is liable for punishment. There are 156 offences in 28 different statutes which are scheduled offences under PMLA. Once the agency concerned with a predicate scheduled offence registers a case, Enforcement Directorate takes up investigations under PMLA to ascertain the proceeds of crime generated from the predicate offence booked by the Law Enforcement Agency. In case a prima-facie case of generation of proceeds of crime and laundering is made out, PMLA provides for seizure and attachment of laundered properties. The action of seizure and attachment is required to be adjudged by the Adjudicating Authority under PMLA.

The persons, both natural and legal entities, who are accused of the offence of money laundering linked to the scheduled offence, can be prosecuted in Special Courts. PMLA provides for rigorous imprisonment of minimum three years which can extend up to seven years and a fine of up to ₹5 lakh on conviction by the Court of persons who have been accused of the offence of money laundering. The conviction can extend up to 10 years if the offence of money laundering is linked to narcotic trafficking. The property attached under PMLA can be confiscated by the Adjudicating Authority after the conviction by the Court of the accused in the trial for scheduled offence.

In terms of PMLA, the tainted proceeds, if found parked overseas, can also be restituted through mutual legal assistance after the collection of such evidence through the process of Letter of Requests with the foreign administration. PMLA also sets out the procedure for reciprocal arrangements with contracting states for seizure, attachment and confiscation of assets found lying overseas. India has signed Mutual Legal Assistance Treaty (MLAT) with 26 countries and by virtue of the provisions of PMLA, Government of India is fully armed with legal measures to get the tainted assets repatriated back to the country on conviction of persons accused of money laundering. Till the conviction, the assets traced overseas can be requested to be seized or frozen by foreign jurisdictions.

Section 12 of PMLA requires financial sector entities (banking companies, financial institutions and intermediaries) to verify the identity of their clients, maintain records and report suspicious/cash transactions (STR/CTR) to FIU-IND. Director, FIU-IND is empowered to conduct inquiry and impose sanctions against financial sector entities for non-compliance with Section 12. Financial Intelligence Unit India (FIU-IND) conducts analysis of information received under PMLA and, in appropriate cases, disseminates information to relevant intelligence/enforcement agencies, which include Central Board of Direct Taxes, Central Board of Excise and Customs, Enforcement Directorate, Narcotics Control Bureau, Central Bureau of Investigation, intelligence agencies and regulators of financial sector.

It may be seen that under both the acts, i.e. FEMA and PMLA, investigation is initiated against specific persons, both natural and legal, and such action is initiated on the basis of specific information.

8.8 Black Money

There is no uniform or accepted definition of 'black' money. Several terms are in use, such as 'black money', 'black income', 'dirty money', 'black wealth', 'underground wealth', 'black economy', 'parallel economy', 'shadow economy', 'underground' or 'unofficial' economy. If money breaks laws in its origin, movement or use, and is not reported for tax purposes, then it would fall within the meaning of *black money*. The broader meaning would encompass and include money derived from corruption and other illegal ways—to include drug trafficking, counterfeiting currency, smuggling, arms trafficking, etc. It would also include all market based legal production of goods and services that are concealed from public authorities for the following reasons:

- To evade payment of taxes (income tax, excise duty, sales tax, stamp duty, etc);
- To evade payment of other statutory contributions;
- To evade minimum wages, working hours and safety standards, etc.; and
- To evade complying with laws and administrative procedures.

There are three sources of black money—crime, corruption and business. The 'criminal' component of black money would normally include proceeds from a range of activities, including racketeering, trafficking in counterfeit and contraband goods, forgery, securities fraud, embezzlement, sexual exploitation and prostitution, drug money, bank frauds and illegal trade in arms. The 'corruption' component of such money would stem from bribery and theft by those holding public office, such as by grant of business, bribes to alter land use or to regularise unauthorised construction, leakages from government social spending programmes, speed money to circumvent or fast-track procedures, black marketing of price controlled services, etc.

8.8.1 Recovery of Black Money

There is a legal framework regulated by the Reserve Bank of India for the opening of bank accounts overseas by Indian residents and for outward or inward remission of funds through authorised channels.

The existing legal framework for dealing with illicitly generated funds transferred overseas and measures for the attachment and repatriation of such illegal assets to India and provision for penalties for offenders are:

- Under the Prevention of Money Laundering Act, 2002 (PMLA), money laundered out of predicate scheduled offences can be attached and seized and individuals and other legal entities found to have indulged in money laundering can be prosecuted. PMLA provides for imprisonment of minimum of 3 years (which can be extended up to 7 years) and a fine of up to ₹5 lakh, and the tainted proceeds parked overseas can be recovered through Mutual Legal Assistance Treaties. India has such treaties with 26 countries.

- Under the Foreign Exchange Management Act, 1999 (FEMA), cases relating to contravention in foreign exchange transactions by Indian residents can be adjudicated with penalty up to a maximum of 3 times the amount involved. Further, FEMA empowers the confiscation of the amounts lying abroad and directing their repatriation.
- Under both statutes (FEMA and PMLA), investigation is taken up against specific persons, both natural and legal, and on the basis of specific information.
- Section 105A of the CrPC provides for reciprocal arrangement and procedure for attachment and forfeiture of properties generated from the commission of an offence. Where such properties are situated overseas and treaty arrangements exist between Government of India and the other country, Letter Rogatories can be issued to a court/ authority of the other country for execution of such an order.
- Under the Income Tax Act also, income earned and not disclosed is taxable and also subject to penalty and interest, as well as prosecution. The amount recovered may even exceed the entire undisclosed income.

➤ 8.8.2 Strategy to Tackle Black Money

The strategy to tackle black money includes:

- Preventing generation of black money
- Discouraging use of black money
- Effective detection of black money
- Effective investigation and adjudication
- Regulated use of large denomination

➤ 8.9 Maharashtra Control of Organised Crime Act (MCOCA), 1999

Maharashtra Control of Organised Crime Act, 1999 (MCOCA) is a law enacted by Maharashtra in 1999 to combat organised crime and terrorism. The preamble to MCOCA says that 'the existing legal framework, i.e., the penal and procedural laws and the adjudicatory system, are found to be rather inadequate to curb or control the menace of organised crime. Government has, therefore, decided to enact a special law with stringent and deterrent provisions including, in certain circumstances, power to intercept wire, electronic or oral communication to control the menace of organised crime. Unlike normal law, the confessions before senior police officers are admissible, not only against the accused giving the confession but also against the other accused in the same case. There is no provision for granting anticipatory bail for six months to the accused.

MCOCA puts a bar on soft liberal bail provisions. Under MCOCA, 'not bail but jail' is the controlling principle. Police can file charge sheet within 180 days instead of the 90 days time limit in normal cases. There are measures in MCOCA which ensure protection of witnesses, like keeping the identity and address of the witness secret, and the witness need not be produced in court.

Probable Questions Based on this Chapter

1. What do you understand by transnational organised crime?
2. What is the interconnection between terrorism and organised crime?
3. What are the main differences between terrorism and organised crime?
4. How is terrorism thriving under the cloak of organised crime in the north-eastern part of India?
5. Write a short note on Money Laundering and Prevention of Money Laundering Act (PMLA).
6. What is black money and how to tackle the menace of black money?

CHAPTER 9

Cyber Security and Role of Social Media

9.1 What is Cyber Security?

Cyber security can be defined as the protection of systems, networks and data in cyber space. It refers to the preventative methods used to protect information from being stolen, compromised or attacked.

Cyber security is a complex issue that cuts across multiple domains and calls for multi-dimensional, multi-layered initiatives and responses. It has proved to be a challenge for governments because it involves various ministries and departments. It is more difficult primarily due to the diffused and varied nature of the threats and the inability to frame an adequate response in the absence of tangible perpetrators.

Cyberspace has expanded dramatically in its brief existence due to rapid development of information technology (IT) and commercial applications associated with it. Advances in information and communications technologies have revolutionised the scientific, educational and commercial infrastructures developed by the government. The IT infrastructure has become an integral part of the critical infrastructure which supports national capabilities such as energy, power grids, telecommunications, emergency communication systems, financial systems, defence systems, space, transport, land records, public essential services and utilities, law enforcement and security and air traffic control networks, to name a few. All these infrastructures increasingly depend on relay data for communication and commercial transactions. The operational stability and security of critical information infrastructure is vital for the economic security of the country.

The evolving nature of the telecommunications infrastructure poses further challenges. The expanding wireless connectivity to individual computers and networks is making determination of physical and logical boundaries of networks increasingly difficult. The increasing inter connectivity and accessibility to computer based systems that are critical to the country's economy are adding to the risk.

9.2 Cyber Threats

Cyber threats vary from simple hacking of an email to waging a war against a state. Cyber threats can be classified broadly into two categories:

1. Cyber crime: against individuals, corporates, etc.
2. Cyber warfare: against a state

9.2.1 Cyber Crime

Use of cyber space, i.e. computer, internet, cellphone, other technical devices, etc., to commit a crime by an individual or organised group is called cyber crime. Cyber attackers use numerous vulnerabilities in cyberspace to commit cybercrime. They exploit the weaknesses in the software and hardware design through the use of malware. *DoS* attacks are used to overwhelm the targeted websites. *Hacking* is a common way of piercing the defences of protected computer systems and interfering with their functioning. *Identity theft* is also common. The scope and nature of threats and vulnerabilities is multiplying with every passing day.

Cyber crimes may be divided into two categories:

1. Crimes that Target Computers Directly

They include:

- Spreading computer viruses
- Denial-of-service (DoS) attack is an attempt to make a machine or network resource unavailable to its intended users. It temporarily or indefinitely interrupts or suspends services of a host connected to the internet.
- Malware (malicious code) is software used to disrupt computer operation, gather sensitive information, or gain access to private computer systems. It can appear in the form of code, scripts, active content, and other software. 'Malware' is a general term used to refer to a variety of forms of hostile or intrusive software, for example Trojan Horses, rootkits, worms, adware, etc.

2. Crimes Facilitated by Computer Networks or Devices, the Primary Target of which is Independent of the Computer Network or Device

This can take many forms as listed below:

- Economic frauds to destabilise the economy of a country, attack on banking transaction system, extract money through fraud, acquisition of credit/debit card data, financial theft and intellectual theft of property
- Impairing the operations of a website or service through data alteration, data destruction
- Spreading pornography
- Copyright infringement
- Cyber stalking, outraging modesty of women, obscene content to humiliate girls and harm their reputation
- Threatening e-mail
- Assuming fake identity, virtual impersonation
- Breach of right to privacy
- Misuse of social media in fanning intolerance, instigating communal tensions and inciting riots. Posting inflammatory material that tends to incite hate-crimes (Even Prime Minister Manmohan Singh expressed deep concern on misuse of social media in sparking off communal sentiments in September)
- Information warfare
- Phishing scams

➤ 9.2.2 Key Terms of Cyber Attack

- **Phishing:** Phishing is the act of attempting to acquire information, such as usernames, passwords and credit card details (and sometimes, indirectly, money) by masquerading as a trustworthy entity in an electronic communication. Communications purporting to be from popular social websites, auction sites, banks, online payment processors or IT administrators are commonly used to lure unsuspecting public. Phishing emails may contain links to websites that are infected with malware. Phishing is typically carried out by email spoofing or instant messaging.
- **Vishing (Voice Phishing):** The term is a combination of 'voice' and 'phishing'. When phishing is done with the help of telephonic system, it is called vishing.
- **Tabnabbing:** Tabnabbing is one of the latest phishing technologies. It takes advantage of tabbed browsing(which uses multiple open tabs) that a user uses and silently redirects the user to the affected site. This technique operates in reverse to most phishing techniques as it does not directly take the user to the fraudulent site, but, instead, phishers load their fake page in one of the open tabs.
- **Whaling:** Several recent phishing attacks have been directed specifically at senior executives and other high profile targets within businesses, and the term whaling has been coined for these kinds of attacks.

- **Spoofing:** A spoofing attack is a situation in which one person or programme successfully masquerades as another by falsifying data and thereby gaining an illegitimate advantage. A spoofing attack involves one programme, system or website successfully masquerading as another by falsifying data and thereby being treated as a trusted system by a user or another programme. The purpose of this is usually to fool programmes, systems or users into revealing confidential information, such as user names and passwords, to the attacker.
- **Zombies:** A zombie is a computer connected to the internet that has been compromised by a hacker, computer virus or trojan horse. It can be used to perform malicious tasks under remote direction. Botnets of zombie computers are often used to spread email spam and launch denial-of-service attacks. Most owners of zombie computers are unaware that their system is being used in this way. Because the owner tends to be unaware, these computers are metaphorically compared to zombies.
- **Botnets:** A botnet is a collection of internetconnected programmes communicating with other similar programmes in order to perform tasks.

  Botnets sometimes compromise computers whose security defences have been breached and control conceded to a third party. Each such compromised device, known as a 'bot', is created when a computer is penetrated by software from a malware (malicious software) distribution.
- **Pharming:** It is an attack to redirect a website's traffic to a different, fake website, where the individual's information is then compromised.
- **Drive-by:** These are opportunistic attacks against specific weaknesses within a system.
- **MITM:** 'Man in the middle attack' is an attack where a middleman impersonates each endpoint and is thus able to manipulate both victims.
- **Spam:** The unsolicited sending of bulk email for commercial purposes, is unlawful in some jurisdictions. While anti-spam laws are relatively new, limits on unsolicited electronic communications have existed for some time.

➤ 9.2.3 Cyber Warfare and Cyber Terror

It is said that future wars will not be like traditional wars which are fought on land, water or air. Snowden revelations have shown that Cyberspace could become the theatre of warfare in the 21st century.

While there is no agreed definition of cyber warfare but 'when any state initiates the use of internet based invisible force as an instrument of state policy to sabotage and espionage against another nation, it is called cyber war'. Attacking the information systems of other countries for espionage and for disrupting their critical infrastructure may be referred as cyber warfare. It includes hacking of vital information, important webpages, strategic controls and intelligence.

The attacks on the websites of Estonia in 2007 and of Georgia in 2008 have been widely reported. Although there is no clinching evidence of the involvement of a state in these attacks, it is widely held that in these attacks, non-state actors (for example, hackers) may have been used by state actors. Since these cyber attacks, the issue of cyber warfare has assumed urgency in the global media.

When an organisation, working independently of a nation state, operates terrorist activities through the medium of cyber space, it is generally called cyber terror.

Special Features of Cyber War Compared to Traditional War

1. **Independent theatre of war:** The development of the internet and low-cost wireless communication is the contemporary equivalent of what airplanes were a hundred years ago. Their use in economic, social and political transactions has increased at a rate that far exceeds the growth in airplane use over the last century. These technologies already play an important part in military operations in the traditional spheres of land, sea, air and the newer one of space. There are signs that they have been used for aggressive purposes by some states. There is also ample evidence of their use by criminals and terrorist groups. It is only a matter of time, like air power a hundred years ago, before cyberspace becomes an independent theatre of war.

   There is one important nuance in the treatment of cyberspace as a fifth potential theatre of war, along with land, sea, air and space. The use of cyberspace depends on physical facilities like undersea cables, microwave and optical fibre networks, telecom exchanges, routers, data servers, and so on. Protecting or attacking these is in the domain of the traditional arms of the military. Cyberspace, as an independent theatre of war, is about attacks that compromise the capability to use these facilities—they cannot be prevented by the security services in isolation.
2. **An undefined space (no specific areas):**The defence of cyberspace has a special feature. The national territory or space that is being defended by the land, sea and air forces is well defined. Outer space and cyberspace are different. They are inherently international even from the perspective of national interest. It is not possible for a country to ignore what is happening in any part of this space if it is to protect the functionality of the cyberspace relevant for its own nationals. Moreover, a key part of this space, the global internet system, is still under the control of one country. Hence, national defence and international cooperation are inevitably intermeshed. This means that a country's government must ensure coherence between its security policy and the diplomatic stance taken by it in multilateral and bilateral discussions on matters like internet and telecom governance, human rights related to information freedoms, trade negotiations on infotech services, and so on.
3. **Disguised attackers:** There is another feature of cyberspace that complicates the design of security structures and policies compared to the other theatres of conflict. In cyberspace, it is very easy for an attacker to cover his tracks and even mislead the target into believing that the attack has

come from somewhere else. This difficulty in identifying the perpetrator makes it difficult to rely on the capacity to retaliate as a deterrent.

4. **No Contact war:** The evolution of technology impacts the nature of conflict and war. Amongst the recent aspects of conflict is 'no contact war' wherein there is no 'physical' or 'kinetic' action across borders.

Future world war will most likely be cyber war. Future war will not be like traditional wars which were fought on territorial borders or in air space.

9.3 Snowden Revelations

Edward Joseph Snowden is an American computer professional, former employee of the Central Intelligence Agency (CIA) and former contractor for the National Security Agency (NSA).

He hogged international limelight when he disclosed to several media outlets thousands of classified documents. Snowden's release of classified material has been described as the most significant leak in US history. The US Department of Justice charged Snowden with espionage.

Snowden's leaked documents uncovered the existence of numerous global surveillance programmes; many of them run by the NSA with the cooperation of telecommunication companies and European governments. The massive extent of NSA's spying, both foreign and domestic, was revealed to the public in a series of detailed disclosures of internal NSA documents. In 2013, the existence of the 'Boundless Informant' was revealed, along with the PRISM electronic data mining programme, the XKeyscore analytical tool, the Tempora interception project, the MUSCULAR access point and the massive FASCIA database, which contains trillions of device-location records. In the following year, Britain's Joint Threat Research Intelligence Group was revealed, along with the Dishfire database, Squeaky Dolphin's real-time monitoring of social media networks and the bulk collection of private webcam images via the Optic Nerve programme.

The disclosures have fuelled debates over mass surveillance, government secrecy and the balance between national security and information privacy.

Modus Operandi of Widespread Cyber Snooping by National Security Agency (NSA)

Basically, three major players were used by the NSA:

- Different nations
- Domestic/foreign agencies
- Private players within and outside the USA

Data was collected through:

- Telecom operators from Global Optic Fibre Network
- Servers of US based internet giants like Google and Microsoft

- Hardware manufacturers like Cisco and Juniper
- Large scale Malware operations and Firewall
- Off the Air components, including Wi-Fi, GSM, CDMA and Satellite signals in alliance with Australia, New Zealand and South Africa
- Taps placed on undersea cables in South America, North of Africa and the Indian Ocean
- Monitoring international payments, banking transactions
- iPhones, Blackberry and Android operating system

Vulnerability of Indian Cyber Space

Documents leaked by NSA whistle-blower Edward Snowden indicate that much of the NSA surveillance was focused on India's domestic politics and its strategic and commercial interests, exposing India's vulnerability to cyber snooping in all sectors. India was fifth among targeted countries. The US has had a major influence on the development of cyberspace by virtue of the fact that much of the initial infrastructure and use was centred in that country and it continues to be a major force in its development and use. The US has thus been in a position to fend off periodic attempts to challenge its supremacy, and those times when it could not, it has been forced to shed some of its control.

➤ 9.3.1 Impact of Snowden Revelations

1. It will pave way for the 'Internet Governance Era'. Microsoft recently allowed foreign customers to have their personal data stored on servers outside America. Hence, the consequence of Edward Snowden's NSA leaks is that countries and companies would erect borders of sorts in cyberspace.
2. Following the shocking revelations about governments' widespread monitoring of global communications, it is clear that all facets of the cybersecurity world have been indelibly changed, from ordinary people having their eyes opened to what is really going on, to governments becoming ever-more distrustful of each other.
3. Some experts believe the technical details contained in documents leaked by Snowden had weakened the security situation in western countries, decreasing the level of security in the US and UK in particular. They feel the leaks were a 'gift' to allow terrorists to 'evade us and strike at will'. It is being said that as fallout of the revelations, Al-Qaeda has changed the way it communicates.
4. One of the biggest impacts Snowden has had on the world is that his leaks have led to an acceleration of cyber arms race around the world.

There is a greater awareness among the masses about the right to privacy. People have become conscious. Even Barack Obama, President of USA, conceded that those leaks triggered a passionate and welcome debate about American snooping.

9.4 Threat to India's Cyber Space

As is clear from Snowden's revelations, India's cyber space is almost unprotected. Till now, we only have very basic security features. We have started considering advanced features only after the Snowden revelations. All our vital institutions, installations and critical infrastructure need to be protected from cyber attacks.

The future war will target crucial areas like:

- Defence installations
- Sensitive documents related to both internal and external security
- Communication networks, including satellites
- ATC management
- Railway traffic control
- Financial services
- Premier institutions of science, technology and research

9.4.1 Critical Infrastructure (CI) and Critical Information Infrastructure (CII)

In general, critical infrastructure (CI) can be defined as:

'Those facilities, systems, or functions, whose incapacity or destruction would cause a debilitating impact on national security, governance, economy and social well-being of a nation.'

It broadly includes the following sectors:

- Energy
- Transportation (air, surface, rail and water)
- Banking and finance
- Telecommunication
- Defence
- Space
- Law enforcement, security and intelligence
- Sensitive government organisations
- Public health
- Water supply
- Critical manufacturing
- E-governance

Across the world, critical information infrastructure (CII) is broadly defined as including 'those networks which are interrelated, interconnected and interdependent'. In India, the guidelines would initially include information and communications, transportation, energy, finance, technology, law enforcement, security and law enforcement, government, space and sensitive organisations.

Critical Information Infrastructure (CII) are those ICT infrastructure upon which the core functionality of critical infrastructure is dependent.

India's new guidelines are an extension of the legislative recognition under the IT Act 2000. Section 70 of the Act defines critical information infrastructure (CII) as:

'Those computer resource and incapacitation or description of which, shall have debilitating impact on national security, economy, public health or safety.'

CII is highly complex, distributed, interconnected and interdependent.

Threats to CII

Threats to CII are classified as:

- *Internal threat*: It is defined as 'one or more individuals with the access and/or inside knowledge of a company, organisation or enterprise that would allow them to exploit the vulnerabilities of that entity's security, systems, services, products or facilities with the intent to cause harm'.

  Insider betrayals cause losses due to IT sabotage, fraud and theft of confidential or proprietary information. This may be intentional or due to ignorance.
- *External threat*: This threat arises from outside of the organisation, by individuals, hackers, organisations, terrorists, foreign government agents, non-state actors, and pose risk, like crippling CII, espionage, cyber/electronic warfare, cyber terrorism, etc.

Threat may be caused by individuals, including disgruntled or former employees, rivals (industrial espionage), hackers, script kiddies, crackers, cyber criminals (organised as well as unorganised), cyber mercenaries, terrorist groups (cyberjehadis), non-state actors and hostile states.

Effects of cyber attacks on CII:

- Damage or destruction of CII
- Disruption or degradation of services
- Loss of sensitive and strategic information
- Widespread damage in short time
- Cascading effects on several CII

9.5 Steps Taken by the Government of India

The following steps have been taken by the Government of India:

- The government has identified a list of critical computer infrastructure which need special protection against cyber attacks. Included in this list are networks related to national security, defence, banks, stock markets, power grids, railways and airlines, weather and many others.
- A national policy on cyber security was framed in 2013.
- A National Critical Information Infrastructure Protection Centre (NCIIPC) is in the process of being set up to create a fool-proof firewall around these networks.

- The creation of NCIIPC is just one of the many ideas being implemented as part of the Framework for Cyber Security that was recently approved by the Cabinet Committee on Security.
- A multi-agency National Cyber Coordination Centre to make assessment of cyber threats and share information with stakeholders is also being set up.
- A Centre of Excellence in Cryptology, the science of encrypting data, is being established at the Indian Institute of Statistics in Kolkata.
- Attacks on Indian networks have come mainly from computers based in 20 countries, including the US, UK, Germany, France, Brazil, Poland and the Netherlands. One such attempt tried to jeopardise the Delhi Commonwealth Games in 2010. Hackers had tried to get into the computer systems to tamper with the timers and scoring machines.
- The government had come up with a 'roadmap on cyber security', that has laid stress on collaboration between the government and private sector in this area.
- As a follow-up to that, the government has set up three cyber-forensic laboratories in Bangalore, Pune and Kolkata in association with the software industry group NASSCOM. Nine more such laboratories are planned in partnership with state governments.
- A cyber crisis management plan has already been put in place, with state governments as an integral part.
- CERT-In, or Computer Emergency Response Team (India), the nodal agency to deal with such crisis is being replicated on a smaller scale for specific sectors.
- The defence establishment has already set up a sectoral CERT for itself. Railways and the power sector are also planning to have a CERT of their own.

➤ 9.5.1 National Cyber Security Policy 2013

Department of Electronics and Information Technology (DeitY) under the Ministry of Communication and Information Technology, Government of India released the National Cyber Security Policy 2013 to build a secure and resilient cyber space for citizens, businesses and government.

The mission of this policy is to (1) protect information and information infrastructure in cyberspace, (2) build capabilities to prevent and respond to cyber threat, (3) reduce vulnerabilities and (4) minimise damage from cyber incidents through a combination of institutional structures, people, processes, technology and cooperation.

The objectives of this policy are defined below.

Objectives

1. To create a secure cyber ecosystem in the country, generate adequate trust and confidence in IT systems and transactions in cyberspace and thereby enhance adoption of IT in all sectors of the economy

2. To create an assurance framework for design of security policies and for promotion and enabling actions for compliance to global security standards and best practices by way of conformity assessment (product, process, technology and people)
3. To strengthen the regulatory framework for ensuring a secure cyberspace ecosystem
4. To enhance and create national and sectoral level 24 x 7 mechanisms for obtaining strategic information regarding threats to ICT infrastructure, creating scenarios for response, resolution and crisis management through effective predictive, preventive, protective, response and recovery actions
5. To enhance the protection and resilience of nation's critical information infrastructure by operating a 24x7 **National Critical Information Infrastructure Protection Centre** (NCIIPC) and mandating security practices related to the design, acquisition, development, use and operation of information resources
6. To develop suitable indigenous security technologies through frontier technology research, solution oriented research, proof of concept, pilot development, transition, diffusion and commercialisation leading to widespread deployment of secure ICT products / processes in general and specifically for addressing national security requirements
7. To improve visibility of the integrity of ICT products and services by establishing infrastructure for testing and validation of security of such products
8. To create a workforce of 5,00,000 professionals skilled in cyber security in the next 5 years through capacity building, skill development and training
9. To provide fiscal benefits to businesses for adoption of standard security practices and processes
10. To enable protection of information while in process, handling, storage and transit so as to safeguard privacy of citizen's data and for reducing economic losses due to cyber crime or data theft
11. To enable effective prevention, investigation and prosecution of cyber crime and enhancement of law enforcement capabilities through appropriate legislative intervention
12. To create a culture of cyber security and privacy enabling responsible user behaviour and actions through an effective communication and promotion strategy
13. To develop effective public private partnerships and collaborative engagements through technical and operational cooperation and contribution for enhancing the security of cyberspace
14. To enhance global cooperation by promoting shared understanding and leveraging relationships for furthering the cause of security of cyberspace
15. To encourage all organisations, private and public, to designate a member of senior management as **Chief Information Security Officer (CISO)**, responsible for cyber security efforts and initiatives

16. To encourage all organisations to develop information security policies duly integrated with their business plans and implement such policies as per international best practices. Such policies should include establishing standards and mechanisms for secure information flow (while in process, handling, storage and transit), crisis management plan, proactive security posture assessment and forensically enabled information infrastructure
17. To ensure that all organisations earmark a specific budget for implementing cyber security initiatives and for meeting emergency response arising out of cyber incidents
18. To provide fiscal schemes and incentives to encourage entities to install, strengthen and upgrade information infrastructure with respect to cyber security
19. To prevent occurrence and recurrence of cyber incidents by way of incentives for technology development, cyber security compliance and proactive actions
20. To establish a mechanism for sharing information and for identifying and responding to cyber security incidents and for cooperation in restoration efforts
21. To encourage entities to adopt guidelines for procurement of trustworthy ICT products and provide for procurement of indigenously manufactured ICT products that have security implications.

Main Features

The main features of the National Cyber Security Policy 2013 include:

1. To promote adoption of global best practices in information security and compliance and thereby enhance cyber security posture
2. To create and maintain testing infrastructure and facilities for IT security product evaluation and compliance verification as per global standards and practices
3. To create awareness of the threats, vulnerabilities and consequences of breach of security among entities for managing supply chain risks related to IT (products, systems or services) procurement
4. To foster education and training programmes both in formal and informal sectors to support the nation's cyber security needs and build capacity
5. To establish cyber security training infrastructure across the country by way of public private partnership arrangements
6. To establish institutional mechanisms for capacity building for law enforcement agencies
7. To promote and launch a comprehensive national awareness programme on security of cyberspace
8. To sustain security literacy awareness and publicity campaign through electronic media to help citizens to be aware of the challenges of cyber security
9. To create a think tank for cyber security policy inputs, discussion and deliberations

10. To develop bilateral and multi-lateral relationships in the area of cyber security with other countries
11. To enhance national and global cooperation among security agencies, CERTs, defence agencies and forces, law enforcement agencies and the judicial systems
12. To create mechanisms for dialogue related to technical and operational aspects with industry in order to facilitate efforts in recovery and resilience of systems, including critical information infrastructure.

Assessment of National Cyber Security Policy (NCSP) 2013

- Security risks associated with Cloud Computing have not been addressed.
- There is also a need to incorporate cyber crime tracking, cyber forensic capacity building and creation of a platform for sharing and analysis of information between public and private sectors on continuous basis.

➤ 9.5.2 National Critical Information Infrastructure Protection Centre (NCIIPC)

The Government is setting up the National Critical Information Infrastructure Protection Centre (NCIIPC) which will function as a specialised unit under the National Technical Research Organisation (NTRO). Under Section 70A of the IT Act, NCIIPC, under NTRO, is being declared as the nodal agency for protection of critical information infrastructure of India.

NCIIPC, under its mandate from Section 70A(2) of IT Act, is responsible for all measures including research and development for protection of critical information infrastructure.

NCIIPC's vision is 'To facilitate safe, secure and resilient information Infrastructure for Critical Sectors of the Nation'.

NCIIPC mission is 'To take all necessary measures to facilitate protection of Critical Information Infrastructure from unauthorised access, modification, use, disclosure, disruption, incapacitation or destruction through coherent coordination, synergy and raising information security awareness among all stakeholders'.

Functions [C]

The functions of NCIIPC include:

1. Identification of critical sub-sectors
2. Study of information infrastructure of identified critical sub-sectors
3. Issue of daily/monthly cyber alerts/advisories
4. Malware analysis
5. Tracking zombies and Malware spreading IPs
6. Cyber forensics activities
7. Research and development for smart and secure environment
8. Facilitate CII owners in adoption of appropriate policies, standards, best practices for protection of CII

9. Annual CISO Conference for critical sectors
10. Awareness and training
11. 24X7 operation and helpdesk

NTRO has identified 17 sub-sectors initially and has started activities for 7 sub-sectors and organisations named below:

- Air traffic management (ATM), Civil aviation (Transportation)
- Power grid (Energy)
- MTNL
- NSEI
- BSNL
- Railways
- SBI

Each organisation/ministry in critical sector should nominate a Nodal Officer (CISO) for interaction with NCIIPC. CISO will be the point of contact for NCIIPC.

➤ Role and Responsibilities of Chief Information Security Officer (CISO)

CISO responsibilities include, but are not limited to:

- Build an Information security culture
- Assist senior management in the development, implementation and maintenance of an information security infrastructure
- Develop, communicate and ensure compliance with organisational information security policy, standards and guidelines
- Ensure regulatory and standards compliance
- Develop a security awareness and training programme
- Periodically conduct internal audit to check compliance with organisational security policy, standard and guidelines
- Risk management
- Incident management
- Business continuity management
- Assist senior management in acquisition of products, tools and services related to information and related technology

➤ 9.5.3 National Telecom Security Policy (NTSP)

NTSP has been formulated with a view to build-in the security features in the systems, services, technologies, equipment, devices and software rather than being an add-on feature. It is a structured policy to deal with issues related to the requirement of the security agencies and to secure the telecom network in the country. It deals with the four broad issues of communication assistance to security agencies, security of communication, information and data, security of telecom network and disaster management. NTSP puts emphasis on indigenisation of sophisticated telecom equipment so that they could be produced and installed in secure environment with all checks and balances.

➤ 9.5.4 Electronic System and Design and Manufacturing (ESDM) Sector Policy

Background of Electronics Industry

At the current rate of growth, domestic production can cater to a demand of USD 100 billion in 2020 as against a demand of USD 400 billion and the rest would have to be met by imports. This aggregates to a demand supply gap of nearly USD 300 billion by 2020. Unless the situation is corrected, it is likely that by 2020, electronics import may far exceed oil imports. This fact goes unnoticed because electronics, as a 'meta resource' forms a significant part of all machines and equipment imported, which are classified in their final sectoral forms, for example, automobiles, aviation, health equipment, media and broadcasting, defence armaments, etc.

Our electronic age is characterised by high velocity of technological change. Consequently, the lifecycle of products is declining. As a result, the value of design and development in the product has increased quite significantly. Given India's growing strength in chip design and embedded software, the increasing importance of design in product development has potential to make India a favoured destination for Electronic System and Design and Manufacturing (ESDM).

There is an urgent need for domestic production and design of electronic equipment.

India is one of the fastest growing markets of electronics in the world. There is potential to develop the ESDM sector to meet our domestic demand as well as to use the capabilities so created to successfully export ESDM products from the country. The National Policy on Electronics aims to address the issue with the explicit goal of transforming India into a premier ESDM hub.

The strategies include setting up of a National Electronics Mission with industry participation and renaming the Department of Information Technology as Department of Electronics and Information Technology (Deity).

Security Implications of ESDM Policy

The policy is expected to create an indigenous manufacturing ecosystem for electronics in the country. It will foster the manufacturing of indigenously designed and manufactured chips creating a more cyber secure ecosystem in the country. It will enable India to tap the great economic potential that this knowledge sector offers. The increased development and manufacturing in the sector will lead to greater economic growth through more manufacturing and consequently greater employment in the sector.

ESDM is of strategic importance as well. Not only in internal security and defence, the pervasive deployment of electronics in civilian domains such as telecom, power, railways, civil aviation, etc. can have serious consequences of disruption of service. This renders tremendous strategic importance to the sector. The country, therefore, cannot be totally dependent on imported electronic components and products.

The policy proposes the following strategies:

(i) *Creating ecosystem for globally competitive ESDM sector*: The strategies include provision of fiscal incentives for investment, setting up of electronic manufacturing clusters, preferential market access to domestically manufactured electronic products, setting up of semiconductor wafer fabrication facilities, industry friendly and stable tax regime. Based on Cabinet approval, a high level empowered committee has been constituted to identify and shortlist technology and investors for setting up two semiconductor wafer manufacturing fabrication facilities. Based on another Cabinet approval a policy for providing preference to domestically manufactured electronic goods has been announced. Separate proposals have also been considered by the Cabinet for approval of Modified Special Incentive Package for the ESDM Sector and for setting up of Electronics Manufacturing Clusters (EMCs).

(ii) *Promotion of exports*: The strategies include aggressive marketing of India as an investment destination and providing incentives for export.

(iii) *Human resource development*: The strategies include involvement of private sector, universities and institutions of learning for scaling up of requisite capacities at all levels for the projected manpower demand. A specialised institute for semiconductor chip design is also proposed.

(iv) *Setting up standards*: Developing and mandating standards to curb inflow of sub-standard and unsafe electronic products by mandating technical and safety standards which conform to international standards.

(v) *Cyber security*: To create a complete secure cyber ecosystem in the country, through suitable design and development of indigenous appropriate products through frontier technology/product oriented research, testing and validation of security of products.

(vi) *Strategic electronics:* The strategies include creating long-term partnerships between domestic ESDM industry and strategic sectors for sourcing products domestically and providing Defence Offset obligations for electronic procurements through ESDM products.

(vii) *Research and development*: Creating ecosystem for vibrant innovation and R&D in the ESDM sector, including nanoelectronics. The strategy includes creation of an Electronic Development Fund.

(viii) *Electronics in other sectors*: The strategy includes supporting and developing expertise in electronics in the following sectors of economy: automotive, avionics, light emitting diodes (LEDs), industrial, medical, solar photovoltaic, information and broadcasting, telecommunications, railways, intelligent transport systems and games and toys.

(ix) *Handling e-waste*: The strategy includes various initiatives to facilitate environment friendly e-waste handling policies.

9.6 Legal Framework

9.6.1 Information Technology Act 2000 (Amended in 2008)

Information technology Act 2000 consists of 94 sections segregated into 13 chapters. The Act was amended in 2008 which has now 124 sections. Salient features of the IT Act are as follows:

1. The Act provides legal recognition to e-commerce, which facilitates commercial e-transactions.
2. It recognises records kept in electronic form like any other documentary record. In this way, it brings electronic transactions at par with paper transactions in documentary form.
3. The Act also provides legal recognition to digital signatures which need to be duly authenticated by the certifying authorities.
4. Cyber Law Appellate Tribunal has been set up to hear appeal against adjudicating authorities.
5. The provisions of the IT Act have no application to negotiable instruments, power of attorney, trust, will and any contract for sale or conveyance of immovable property.
6. The Act applies to any cyber offence or contravention committed outside India by a person irrespective of his/her nationality.
7. As provided under Section 90 of the Act, the State Government may, by notification in 'Official Gazette', make rules to carry out the provisions of the Act.
8. Consequent to the passing of this Act, the SEBI had announced that trading of securities on the internet will be valid in India, but initially there was no specific provision for protection of confidentiality and net trading. This lacuna has been removed by the IT (Amendment) Act, 2008.

9.6.2 Offences under the IT Act

Sec-65. Tampering with Computer Source Documents

Whoever knowingly or intentionally conceals, destroys, or alters any computer source code used for a computer, computer program, computer system or computer network, when the source code is required to be kept or maintained by law, shall be punishable with imprisonment up to three years, or with fine which may extend up to two lakh rupees, or with both.

Sec-66. Hacking with Computer System

1. Whoever with the intent of cause or knowing that is likely to cause, wrongful loss or damage to the public or any person destroys or deletes or alters any information residing in a computer resource or diminishes its value or utility or affects it injuriously by any means, commits hacking.
2. Whoever commits hacking shall be punished with imprisonment up to three years, or with fine which may extend up to two lakh rupees, or with both.

Sec-66-A Sending Offensive Messages through Communication Service, etc. (Introduced Vide Amendment in 2008)

Any person who sends, by means of a computer resource or a communication device,

(a) Any information that is grossly offensive or has menacing character; or
(b) Any information which he knows to be false, but for the purpose of causing annoyance, inconvenience, danger, obstruction, insult, injury, criminal intimidation, enmity, hatred, or ill will, persistently makes by making use of such computer resource or a communication device, or
(c) Any electronic mail or electronic mail message for the purpose of causing annoyance or inconvenience or to deceive or to mislead the addressee or recipient about the origin of such messages shall be punishable with imprisonment for a term which may extend to three years and with fine.

9.7 International Cooperation in Cyber Security

9.7.1 NETmundial Conference 2014

Sau Paulo in Brazil hosted a two-day conference in April 2014 on internet governance. It included representatives from nearly 180 countries. Its theme was 'Global Multi-stakeholder Meeting on the Future of Governance'.

A global discussion on Net governance tried to bring the vision of multiple stakeholders in line with democracy. India took this opportunity to highlight US dominance of the internet and press for equal rights and say for all nations on matters related to Internet governance and cyber security. India lamented the lack of truly representative and democratic nature of the existing systems of internet governance, including the management of critical internet resources, and called for cyber jurisprudence to ensure security of the cyberspace.

There are three major issues here.

1. Should internet governance be carried out through a multilateral model or multi-stakeholder model? The multilateral model involves primarily Governments. UN is operated by this model.
   On the other hand, multi-stakeholder model recognizes that civil society groups, internet users and corporates have a say as well. Russia, India and China were in favour of multilateral model. 'Civil society' and Western countries are more inclined towards a multi-stakeholder set-up. While a multi-stakeholder option seems like the more reasonable and politically correct choice, it begs the question: Who are these civil society groups, who do they claim to represent, and how do we know that they simply haven't been hijacked by corporate interests?
2. The second issue is the question of internet fragmentation or 'Balkanisation' of the internet. Western countries and civil society groups fear that as countries such as India and Russia reduce their reliance on American

infrastructure, they will shatter the global unity of the internet and impose barriers that will hinder connections between users in different countries. While this fear is real, it also shuts us off to looking at a different type of Balkanisation; one where we reduce dependence on surveillance-tinged, Silicon Valley-based services while promoting local and secure digital infrastructure. In India, these fault lines are already being drawn, for better or worse: The Election Commission recently aborted a potential partnership with Google, for voter facilitation services, on the grounds of 'national security'. Government officials are slowly starting to shun Hotmail and Gmail as well. Technology start-ups like Wonobo, a Google Street clone, are starting to receive Government backing.

3. Third issue is 'net neutrality' or the principle that telecom companies should treat all internet content equally as it flows through their cables and pipes. If net neutrality is abandoned, internet service providers would be allowed to prioritise certain types of traffic, leading to disastrous consequences.

On most of these issues, and a few others such as intellectual property, NETmundial has scored poorly, mostly because vested interests often take root when the global community has to strive for 'rough consensus'.The conference's outcome document takes soft stances on validating the multi-stakeholder model and condemning surveillance. Net neutrality, for instance, is relegated to a 'point of future discussion'.

The proposal for a decentralised internet assumes significance in the wake of Edward Snowden's Wikileaks revelations of mass surveillance in recent months.

The US has had a major influence on the development of cyberspace by virtue of the fact that much of the initial infrastructure and use was centred in that country and it continues to be a major force in its development and use. The US has thus been in a position to fend off periodic attempts to challenge its supremacy, and those times when it has been forced to shed some of its control.

Bowing to the demands of Brazil and other nations following revelations last year of its massive electronic surveillance of internet users, the United States has agreed to relinquish oversight of the Internet Corporation for Assigned of Names and Numbers (ICANN), a non-profit group based in California that assigns internet domain names or addresses. The revelations by former NSA analyst, Edward Snowden, brought worldwide calls for the United States to reduce its control of the internet, created 50 years ago to link the computers of American universities to the US defence industry.

9.8 Social Media

Social media refers to internet based communication among people who create, share and exchange their ideas, photos, videos and information on virtual cyber platform. Its reach and popularity among people has rapidly increased over the last few years, primarily due to a sharp rise in the number of internet users and cell phone users. It is claimed that people spent more than 20% of the time spent on internet on social media. Nearly 20 crore people use internet in India. It is likely that it will soon overtake US as far as number of internet users is concerned. People freely exercise their right to express on social media as well as they get access to faster information and knowledge. Knowledge is power. Information is power. Social media includes Facebook, Twitter, Youtube, blogs, new microblogging sites, etc.

➤ 9.8.1 How is Social Media different from Traditional Media?

Social Media is a new form of media. It is different from traditional media in the following ways:

1. It rapidly passes information to its users. It is distinct from traditional media because it provides real time communication of information. Information on social media is widely spread within a very short time so its impact is much far than traditional print and electronic media and also far than traditional modes for communication, like telephone, postal and face-to-face communication.
2. Traditional print media and electronic media are controlled by big media houses. Their control is limited to a selected few. So they exercise their monopoly by influencing the masses, elections and politics through modified distorted version of news items. But social media is in the hands of people. It cannot be controlled by any individual or any group. So, social media has broken the monopoly of big media houses. Social media has ensured a greater transparency in traditional media. In fact, electronic media and print media are also becoming available on social media now.
3. Traditional media provides one-way communication. It only provides information to users but people discuss and debate on current issues, important policies, etc. on the social media. So, social media has not only enhanced transparency and accountability of the government, it has also made our democracy more participatory. It has developed a culture of debate that is the most important requirement for strengthening any democracy.

➤ 9.8.2 Negative Usage of Social Media

The negative usage of social media includes:

- Riots
- Misinformation
- Terrorism, anti-national activities
- False opinion building
- Addiction
- Inciting communal violence

➤ 9.8.3 Positive Usage of Social Media

The positive usage of social media includes:

- Social awareness
- Cheapest and fastest form of communication
- Spread of social activism like movements against corruption and sexual harassment, etc.
- Promoting a culture of debate and discussion
- Breaking the monopoly of big media houses
- Participatory democracy

➤ 9.9 Key Issues

Since the last 2-3 years, a debate has been going on regarding use / misuse of social media. On the one hand are the issues of freedom of expression and right of privacy, while on the other, are the issues of hurting religious sentiments, promoting hatred, enmity between different classes & groups, causing annoyance, criminal defamation etc. We know that there has to be a fine balance between the two, while freedom of expression envisaged in the Constitution is the right of individual but we have to exercise it within the limits of law and we have to see that we don't hurt others feeling which creates law and order problems for the administration. We have to take care of the rights of others also.

Two instances that got highlighted in the recent past are given below:

1. The arrest of two women over a comment on Facebook sparked off widespread anger in India. One of the women, in her Facebook post, had criticized the shutdown of Mumbai after the death of politician Bal Thackeray, while the other had 'liked' the comment. The women accused of 'promoting enmity between classes' were later released on bail. It sparked a nationwide debate of Section 66-A of IT Act 2000. The chairman of the Press Council of India Markandey Katju, also criticized the arrests. Later, the charges against the girls were withdrawn by the Government.
2. Aseem Trivedi, a cartoonist, was arrested on the charge of putting seditious cartoons on Facebook. Although his cartoons were related to corruption and the failure of the Parliament to deal with corruption, he faced serious allegations of insulting the national emblem, the Parliament, the flag and the Constitution through his anti-corruption cartoons. In January 2012, a case of sedition (Section 124A of the Indian Penal Code) was filed against him in the Beed District Court, Maharashtra. Additional charges were brought against him by the Maharashtra Police in Mumbai for insulting India's national symbols, under the State Emblem of India (Prohibition of Improper Use) Act 2005. He was arrested in Mumbai on September 9, 2012 on charges of sedition, related to the content of his work. This also faced lot of criticism by media.

PROBABLE QUESTIONS BASED ON THIS CHAPTER

1. Explain the following terms:
   (a) Phishing
   (b) Tabnabbing
   (c) Whaling
   (d) Spoofing
   (e) Zombies
   (f) Botnets
2. What are the basic features of the National Cyber Security Policy 2013?
3. What are social networking sites and what security implications do these sites present?
4. What is CII and how is it important for cyber security of India?
5. What are the salient features of NCIIPC?
6. What are the implications of Snowden revelations on cyber security of India?
7. What is cyber war? How is it different from a traditional war?

CHAPTER 10

Security Challenges and Their Management in Border Areas

10.1 Challenges of Border Security

Borders are the visible symbols of a country's sovereignty, unity and integrity. Borders are seen as a symbol of national pride. There are three distinct sets of borders at the international level:

- Land borders
- Maritime boundaries
- Airspace

Border management in the present world order is a complex proposition. The transgressor is always on the lookout for soft gaps on land, along the coast or if need be, from the air. The 1995 Purulia incident has already demonstrated our vulnerability from the air. It is therefore necessary to adopt a holistic approach to border management.

Managing borders is difficult for several reasons. Some of our maritime boundaries are still unsettled. Land borders are not fully demarcated. Sections of our borders are based on artificial boundaries and not natural features.

10.2 India's Land Boundaries with Her Immediate Neighbours

India shares approx. 15,000 kilometres of boundary with her immediate neighbours, namely Pakistan (3,323 km), China (3,488 km), Nepal (1,751 km), Bhutan (699 km), Myanmar (1,643 km) and Bangladesh (4,096 km). India's boundary with each of her neighbours runs through a variety of ecological milieus, each with its own unique setting and associated problems. For example, the India-Pakistan border areas are spread across extreme climatic conditions, given that the boundary runs from the hot Runn of Kuchh to Thar Desert in Rajasthan to the cold Himalayas in Jammu and Kashmir. Similarly, in the north, the India–China boundary runs along one of the loftiest mountain ranges covered with snow all through the year. The India–Myanmar boundary is draped with lush tropical forests with myriad undergrowths. The Indo–Bangladesh boundary has to cope with the ever-shifting riverbeds in the region. These diverse ecological and climatic conditions create immense hurdles for extending the security and administrative reach in these border areas. Coupled with this, the man-made nature of these boundaries also throws up serious issues, such as border disputes, porous borders, continuance of trans-border ethnic and social ties, etc. Together, they pose a serious challenge to the effective management of the borders. Let's examine each of our borders with our neighbouring countries.

10.2.1 Indo–Pakistan Border

The India-Pakistan boundary is categorised under three different heads:

- *Radcliff line*: This is 2,308 km long, stretches from Gujarat to parts of Jammu district in Jammu and Kashmir.
- *Line of Control* (LoC): This line is 776 km long and runs along the districts of Jammu (some parts), Rajouri, Poonch, Baramula, Kupwara, Kargil and some portions of Leh.
- *Actual Ground Position Line* (AGPL): This is 110 km long and extends from NJ 9842 to Indira Col in the North.

The LoC and the AGPL have seen constant tensions with border skirmishes and firing between the armies, and border security forces constantly guarding boundaries of both the countries. The LoC has been vulnerable to constant infiltration by foreign terrorists, Kashmiri separatists and Pakistani army regulars for long.

Like the Bangladesh boundary, the India-Pakistan boundary also does not follow any geographical barrier. It runs through diverse terrain like deserts, marshes, plains and snow clad mountains, and winds its way through villages, houses and agricultural lands, making it extremely porous. Porosity of this border has facilitated various illegal activities, such as smuggling, drugs and arms trafficking, and infiltration. Heroin and fake Indian currency are the two predominant items of smuggling along this border. Other items include saffron, textiles and mercury, which are smuggled from Pakistan. The villagers adjacent to the border are alleged to be involved in smuggling in a big way. Money laundering is also quite rampant along the border. A large scale hawala network is flourishing in Punjab, especially in Ludhiana. In addition, the border population has also been subjected to hostile propaganda by Pakistan, designed to mislead and sway their loyalties. The Sir Creek area, due to its peculiar terrain, makes the movement of border guarding forces very difficult and thus provides scope for illegal fishing in the creeks.

➤ 10.2.2 Indo-China Border

The entire boundary is disputed and is known as 'McMahon Line'. As regards border management, the India-China border throws up only a few challenges. There is hardly any circulation of people or goods between the two countries through the border. The Himalayan range which lies astride the boundary has prevented any large scale trans-border interactions between people residing on either side of the border.

➤ 10.2.3 Indo-Bangladesh Border

India shares the longest border (4,096 km) with Bangladesh. Bangladesh borders the Indian states of West Bengal in the west and north, Assam and Meghalaya in the north-east, and Tripura and Mizoram in the east. The boundary was drawn by 'Bengal Boundary Commission'. Instead of following natural barriers, it meanders through villages, agricultural lands and rivers, rendering the border extremely porous with many disputed pockets. Un-demarcated stretches, existence of enclaves (chhit-mohols), and adverse possessions are cause of constant friction between the border guarding forces of India and Bangladesh.

In 1974, three years after the liberation of Bangladesh, the then prime ministers of India and Bangladesh, Indira Gandhi and Sheikh Mujib-ur-Rahman, inked an agreement to settle the land boundary issue. The Indira-Mujib Agreement laid down the methods for demarcating various disputed stretches of the India-Bangladesh boundary. Under the agreement, India retained the southern half of enclaves and Bangladesh retained the other half.

The Enclave bill pending in Parliament needs to be discussed in detail. At present, there are 111 Indian enclaves in Bangladesh and 51 Bangladeshi enclaves in India. Since India does not have access to these enclaves, it has not been possible to establish administrative set-up to provide facilities like police stations, courts, schools, roads, hospitals, banks, markets, etc. for the residents.

A major consequence of the porous border is the ease with which it is crossed illegally. The trend of illegal migration from Bangladesh into India has continued since independence. Various 'push' factors, such as poverty, political upheavals, religious persecution, demographic pressures and environmental crises, and 'pull' factors, such as availability of land, employment opportunities, medical care and education, have contributed to the large-scale influx of Bangladeshis into India. The porosity of the border also allows Indian insurgents to cross over to Bangladesh and other neighbouring countries for asylum.

Porous border, lack of economic opportunities, poverty and underdevelopment, attitude of the people towards petty crimes, laxity in vigilance, alleged nexus between criminals and police and border guarding forces all contribute to the escalating trans-border crimes.

Smuggling of cattle has become a serious concern. Truckloads of cattle from Haryana, Rajasthan, Uttar Pradesh and Madhya Pradesh are shipped to the India-Bangladesh border everyday, ostensibly for grazing purposes. From here, these cattle are smuggled into Bangladesh. The Border Security Force (BSF) regularly seizes cattle. Along with cattle, smuggling of arms and other essential items, such as sugar, salt and diesel, human and narcotics trafficking, counterfeit Indian currency, kidnapping, and thefts are quite common along this border.

➤ 10.2.4 Indo-Nepal Border

India and Nepal have shared an open border (1,700 Km) since 1950 under the 'Treaty of Peace and Friendship'. There are many points of dispute, mostly a result of the constantly shifting courses of the turbulent Himalayan Rivers (especially Kalapani and Susta). The submergence, destruction and removal of border pillars and encroachment into no-man's land by people from either side add to the problem. Allegations of excesses, such as intimidation and forcible grabbing of land by either side along the disputed border, also surface from time to time. The disputed border has created unease not only between the two countries but also among their local populations. Unrestricted migration over the years has produced territorial pockets dominated by people originating from the other country.

An open border allows easy access to terrorists and insurgents. In the late 1980s, Sikh and Kashmiri terrorists sneaked into India via Nepal. ULFA, NDBF and KLO have misused the open border in the past. Earlier, reportedly, Maoists often escaped into India when pursued by Nepalese security agencies. Apart from insurgents and terrorists, many hard-core criminals pursued by Indian and Nepalese security forces escape across the open border. ISI, LeT and other terrorist organisations are continuously using Nepal as a transit route and are also operating from soil of Nepal. They are taking advantage of the open and porous border.

➤ 10.2.5 Indo-Myanmar Border

The boundary was demarcated in 1967 under an agreement signed by both countries. However, numerous earlier treaties and acts had affected the alignment of portions of the boundary and formed much of the basis of the new agreement.

The location of the Indo-Myanmar border throws up many challenges for its effective management. Though the boundary is properly demarcated, there are a few disputed pockets. The rugged terrain makes movement and overall development of the area difficult. The internal dynamics of the region in terms of clan loyalties of the tribal people, inter-tribal clashes, insurgency and trans-border ethnic ties also adversely affect the security of the border areas. There is practically no physical barrier along the border either in the form of fences or border outposts and roads to ensure strict vigil. Close ethnic ties among the tribes, such as Nagas, Kukis, Chin, etc., who live astride the border, help insurgents in finding safe haven in Myanmar.

The location of the boundary at the edge of the 'golden triangle' facilitates unrestricted illegal inflow of drugs into India. The smuggling of arms and ammunition, precious stones and Chinese made consumer items finds its way into India illegally. Red Sanders, ATS (amphetamine type stimulant), grocery items, bicycle parts, etc. are smuggled from India. Human trafficking is also rampant along the border. The provision of allowing the tribal communities of both countries to travel up to 16 km across the border without any passport or visa called 'Free Movement Regime' has also contributed to increased smuggling in the region.

10.2.6 Indo-Bhutan Border

The boundary is demarcated except along the tri-junction with China, where the boundary is open. The border was peaceful till Indian insurgent groups such as KLO, ULFA and NDBF established camps in the southern districts of Bhutan though these were flushed out later. Taking advantage of the open border, these insurgents would sneak into Bhutan after carrying out extortions, killings and bomb blasts. Smuggling and trafficking are also rampant along the border. Chinese made goods, Bhutanese cannabis, liquor and forest products are major items smuggled into India. Livestock, grocery items and fruits are smuggled to Bhutan.

10.3 Coastal Security and Island Territories

Water channels, most of which are interconnected and run deep inside the land, render the coastline porous and hence vulnerable to cross-border infiltration, smuggling and arms and drugs trafficking. Existence of mangrove forests, sandbars and uninhabited islands along the coast provide ideal hideaways for infiltrators and criminals. In recent years, the use of sea by terrorists to carry out attacks, as was seen during the 1993 Mumbai serial blasts and the November 2008 attack on Mumbai, have also added a new dimension to the vulnerability of the coastline.

The matter is made worse by the existence of several high value targets such as oil refineries, atomic power plants, space stations, ports and naval bases along the coastline. There is growing worry about non-conventional threats as well as terrorist attacks, sabotage, etc., on such targets which could potentially inflict massive damage.

Straying of both Indian and Pakistani fishermen into each other's territorial waters and their subsequent arrests has also been a perennial source of concern. It is feared that at least some of the arrested fishermen could be recruited by Pakistan's Inter Service Intelligence (ISI) and used as agents against India and their boats could be used to sneak in arms, explosives and operatives into India.

Since these boats have Indian make and registration number, they could easily evade attempts by Indian security agencies to track them. This is what seems to have happened when the Coast Guard let off the 'Kuber', the vessel in which the terrorists travelled in November 2008.

Strategic location of the island territories, i.e. their proximity to the important Sea Lanes of Communication (SLOC) and Southeast Asian and African countries, coupled with considerable distance from the mainland add to their vulnerability. In recent years, intelligence reports have suggested that many uninhabited islands are being misused by terrorist groups and criminal gangs as transit points for smuggling arms and narcotics. Internal disturbances in India's neighbouring littoral countries also make the security scenario of the island territories extremely grim. The Andaman and Nicobar islands have seen large scale influx of illegal migrants from Bangladesh, Sri Lanka (Tamils), Myanmar, Thailand and Indonesia. Besides, the Indian Ocean has been a theatre of intense rivalries between great powers, mostly extra-regional powers.

10.4 Challenges to Managing Our Borders

The challenges include:

- Confronting the challenges to the unity and integrity of India
- Upholding our sovereignty
- Defending our territorial jurisdiction
- Preventing infiltration and illegal movement across the border
- Inculcating a sense of safety and freedom among people living in border areas
- Checking trafficking of all kinds (arms, humans, drugs)
- Controlling the trafficking in Fake Currency Indian Notes (FCIN)
- Prevention of smuggling of goods like cattle, gold etc

10.5 Techniques of Effective Border Management

The following techniques would help in managing and securing the borders:

- Building of fences and erecting floodlights
- Creating effective Border outposts (BoP)
- Step-up infrastructure development, like roads
- Effective patrolling and building of observation post towers
- Building of Naka/machan
- Equipping the security forces with night vision technologies
- Installation of CCTV and thermal imaging equipment

10.6 The Kargil Review Committee Report and Its Observations on Border Management

The concept of border management assumed greater importance in the government lexicon only in the wake of the Kargil conflict of 1999, and the subsequent report submitted by the Kargil Review Committee. Based on the recommendations of the Review Committee, the Government of India, in April 2001, set up a 'task force' on border management under the chairmanship of Madhav Godbole. This task force was part of a Group of Ministers (GoM) constituted to review the national security system as a whole and the recommendations of the Kargil Review Committee in particular. The task force's objective was to 'consider measures for border management and, in particular, to consider the recommendations of the Kargil Review Committee in this regard and formulate specific proposals for the GoM's consideration'.

The report observed that the country's borders cannot be effectively managed because of certain inherent problems, such as their disputed nature, artificiality and porosity, which according to it give rise to multiple problems like illegal migration, smuggling, drugs trafficking, and trans-border movement of insurgents. In addition, the multiplicity of forces employed to guard the same border, their repeated withdrawal from the borders for other duties, the lack of adequate infrastructure along the border, etc., prevent them from efficiently guarding the border. To address these vital issues the GoM recommended:

- Concerted efforts are to be made to settle border disputes and demarcate the borders at the earliest opportunity
- 'Department of Border Management' be created
- One border guarding force should be deployed on one border and it should not be distracted from its principal task and deployed for other internal security duties
- Establishment of a marine police force, strengthening of Coast Guard and setting up of an apex institution for coordinating various maritime issues
- Accelerated development of infrastructure along the border, especially to wean away the border population from illegal activities

India's neighbourhood is in turmoil. Several of India's neighbours are undergoing political and economic instability. India also has continuing border disputes with several of her neighbours. Uncertain borders not only raise bilateral tensions but also facilitate cross-border infiltration, illegal migration, smuggling and crime. Of these, illegal migration has emerged as one of the major national security challenges.

The Group of Ministers undertook a thorough review of border management issues and made several recommendations in 2001. Many of these recommendations are being implemented. One of the major recommendations was the setting up of a separate Department of Border Management within the Ministry of Home Affairs. This has been done. Yet, other major recommendations like the early settlement of our maritime borders and the demarcation of land boundaries has not yet been fully implemented. The GoM had strongly recommended the principle of 'one border one force' for better accountability. It emphasised the imperative of not deploying the border guarding forces for law and order duties and counter insurgencies. It made some recommendations specific to better management of India-Pakistan, India-Nepal and other borders. It lamented the neglect of maritime borders and island territories and made recommendations to strengthen coast guard and police. As a result of these recommendations, border management has got more attention but the Mumbai terrorist attacks have once again shown that a lot more needs to be done to improve border management.

In the last two years, India has built several thousand kilometres of fences on India-Bangladesh and India-Pakistan borders. Border guarding forces have been augmented. Several thousand crores of rupees have been spent on their modernisation and expansion. The Government has announced a policy of setting up 13 modern integrated check posts to improve border management. Technology will play a major role in improving border management. We may have to learn how other large countries manage their borders.

Approach to Border Management

The approach as employed by the Government towards managing the borders has four important elements, viz. (a) guarding, (b) regulation, (c) development of border areas, and (d) constituting bilateral institutional mechanisms for resolving disputes and ironing out conflicts with neighbours. We shall examine each one of the above elements.

➤ 10.6.1 Guarding

The BSF has been assigned responsibility for the India-Pakistan and India-Bangladesh borders, Assam Rifles (AR) for the India-Myanmar border, the Indo-Tibetan Border Police (ITBP) for the India-China border, and the Sashastra Seema Bal (SSB) for the India-Nepal and India-Bhutan borders.

For managing the borders effectively, it is important to have better surveillance. Surveillance is carried out by conducting regular patrols by the personnel guarding our borders. To house these personnel and to send regular patrols and to interact with the nearby villages, border out posts (BOP) have been set up all along the borders. The inter-BOP distances along various borders are far greater than the recommended 2.5 km.

For securing the riverine and creek areas along the India-Bangladesh and India-Pakistan borders, the water wing of the BSF is deployed.

In addition, several electronic surveillance equipment like Night Vision Devices, Hand Held Thermal Imagers, Battle Field Surveillance Radars, Direction Finders, Unattended Ground Sensors, High Powered Telescope, etc. are used by the border guarding forces as force multipliers for greater surveillance.

➤ 10.6.2 Regulation

Efficient regulation of movement of people and goods is the hallmark of an effective border management strategy. For this, the government has to facilitate legitimate trade and travel while simultaneously checking illegal migration, infiltration of insurgents and terrorists and prevent smuggling. Building barriers is an effective means and for this fencing is employed but it is not an easy task. Some problem areas are:

- Acquisition of land
- Inordinate delay due to non-cooperation by local bodies
- In many instances, vested interests and state governments try to halt the process due to vote bank politics by illegal migrants

Another method of regulation is issuance of multi-purpose national identity cards and construction of Integrated Check Posts (ICPs) to facilitate legal trade and movement.

➤ 10.6.3 Development of Border Areas

Border areas remain inaccessible and underdeveloped due to difficult terrain and lack of facilities like proper roads, educational institutions and hospitals. Lack of economic opportunities makes the border population more susceptible to take up smuggling and trafficking. Keeping in mind these problems, the Union government initiated the 'border area development programme' (BADP) in 1987 to provide adequate social and economic infrastructure, promote participation in development, eliminate sense of alienation, and instil a sense of security among the border people. BADP schemes comprise of development of community based infrastructure like forestry, pasture land, fishery ponds, floriculture parks, community centres, mobile dispensaries, mini marketing yards, etc. Over the years, the nature of the programme has changed from a schematic one with emphasis on education to a state-level programme with emphasis on balanced development of border areas. Grass-root level institutions such as panchayati raj institutions, district councils/traditional councils are encouraged to participate in deciding the priority schemes for their areas.

North-east India, which shares 98 per cent of its borders with Bhutan, China, Myanmar and Bangladesh, has been plagued by insurgency and under-development. Its strategic location as a gateway to South East Asia has propelled the government to undertake various developmental programmes in recent years. To study the situation of the North-east region and suggest suitable projects for its development, the Government constituted the L C Jain Committee and the high level commission under the chairmanship of S P Shukla in the 1990s. The Commission in its report titled 'Transforming the North-east' noted the inadequate infrastructure in the region and strongly advocated the need to develop them, especially road networks. Consequently, a series of schemes were initiated to develop the road network in the region. Among these, the three most important schemes are National Highway Development Programme Phase II, National Highway Development Programme Phase III B and Special Accelerated Road Development Programme for the North-east Region (SARDP-NE) 2007-2008.

➤ 10.6.4 Constituting Bilateral Institutional Mechanisms

To facilitate bilateral dialogue on matters of mutual concern regarding border management, the Government of India has constituted a system of institutionalised interaction through the meetings of home secretaries, area commanders of border guarding forces and the joint working group on border management. For instance, to discuss issues of insurgency and smuggling along the Indo-Myanmar border, foreign office consultations (FOC) at the level of Foreign Secretary on the Indian side and Deputy Foreign Minister on Myanmar's side take place regularly.

National level meetings (NLMs) and sectoral level meetings (SLM) also take place under the Home Secretary and the Joint Secretary of the Ministry of Home Affairs, respectively. The primary objective of these meetings is 'to maintain peace and tranquillity all along the border' and to attain this objective, the two sides have agreed to 'prevent inadvertent violations of each others' territories by their security forces' and also to 'monitor and curb effectively all illegal and negative activities such as trans-border movement of insurgents, narco-traffickers and others involved in nefarious activities'. Border liaison meetings (BLMs) take place between local Area Army Commanders at designated places every six months.

The Surveyor Generals of India and Myanmar also meet to discuss the work plan for joint inspection, repairs, restoration and maintenance of boundary pillars on the border. India has also constituted similar institutional mechanisms with Bangladesh, Pakistan, Nepal and Bhutan. On Indo-Bangladesh border, several bilateral mechanisms with BGB (Border Guards of Bangladesh) exist, such as Company Commander level meeting, Commandant level meeting, Sector Commander level meeting, Inspector General BSF–Deputy Director General BGB level meeting, Nodal officer level meetings and Director General BSF–Director General BGB level Border Coordination Conference. A similar layered bilateral mechanism with Pakistan Rangers also exists.

These bilateral mechanisms have been helpful in sensitizing each other about their respective security concerns and formulating strategies for better management of the border.

10.7 Securing the Coasts and Island Territories

For securing the coasts, the Government of India has implemented a three-layered mechanism. At the *outermost layer*, the Indian Navy patrols the high seas and carries out aerial reconnaissance with ship-based aircraft. The *intermediate layer* comprising the Exclusive Economic Zone (between 12 and 200 nautical miles) is patrolled by the Coast Guard. The areas around the land-sea interface are patrolled by the Coastal Police. On the recommendation of the Task Force, the Indian government launched the coastal security scheme in 2005-06. The scheme envisaged the establishment of '73 coastal police stations equipped with 204 boats, 153 jeeps and 312 motorcycles for mobility on coast and in close coastal waters' over a period of five years.

Coastal police stations do not have adequate trained manpower, nor sophisticated arms or patrol boats. The personnel deployed in these police stations are reluctant to undertake sea patrolling. They complain of sea sickness, lack of proper training and absence of high speed patrol boats.

Following the Mumbai terror attacks, the government has also announced a series of measures for strengthening coastal security of the country. These include:

- Expediting the implementation of coastal security scheme
- Speedy delivery of 204 interceptor boats
- Easing of environmental norms for setting up coastal police stations

- Issuance of multi-purpose identity cards to all fishermen, sea ferrying personnel and coastal villages
- Implementation of uniform licensing of fishing boats across the country
- Installation of special transponders and global positioning system on registered boats for identification and tracking,
- Deployment of commando units of Central Industrial Security Force in all ports
- Constitution of a unified command for coastal districts to counter terrorist threats from the sea

For the security of the Island Territories, the Indian Government has set up a joint command in the Andaman and Nicobar Islands, called the Andaman and Nicobar Command (ANC), comprising personnel of the Army, the Navy, the Air Force and the Coast Guard. Among other responsibilities, the ANC is also mandated to look after the defence of Andaman and Nicobar Islands.

PROBABLE QUESTIONS BASED ON THIS CHAPTER

1. What are the challenges to border management in India?
2. How far are internal security challenges linked with border management?

CHAPTER

11 Security Forces and Their Mandate

11.1 Central Armed Police Forces (CAPFs)

There are basically two types of central security forces, viz., CAPF and CPMF.

CAPFs stand for Central Armed Police Forces. This new terminology was introduced in 2011 on the request of the Army. Presently the CAPF comprise the following eight police forces of the Union government.

(a) BSF	(b) CRPF	(c) ITBP	(d) CISF
(e) SSB	(f) NSG	(g) SPG	(h) RPF

The first six, viz., BSF, CRPF, ITBP, CISF, SSB and NSG are under the administrative control of the Ministry of Home Affairs (MHA), while the SPG is under the Cabinet Secretariat and the RPF is under the Ministry of Railways. They all are headed by senior IPS officers. Most of the higher posts in these five are filled through deputation by IPS officers. These forces assist and report to MHA. Earlier they were known as Central Paramilitary Forces (CPMF). Out of these five, the first three namely, BSF, SSB, ITBP are basically border guarding forces while the CRPF is for internal security and election duties.

CRPF also provides security to major critical installations of the country. NSG is the commando force meant for counter terrorism but also looks after high risk VIP security. SPG is for proximate security of PM and ex-PM while RPF guards railway property and ensures passenger safety.

➤ 11.1.1 Border Security Force (BSF)

The Border Security Force (BSF) is a border guarding force. It was established on December 1, 1965. Its primary role is to guard India's international borders with Pakistan and Bangladesh during peacetime and also prevent trans-border crime. BSF is headed by an IPS officer and is under the administrative control of the Ministry of Home Affairs (MHA). The Indo-Pakistan war of 1965 demonstrated the inadequacies of the existing border management system and led to the formation of the Border Security Force as a unified central agency with the specific mandate of guarding India's international boundaries with Pakistan. The BSF had trained, supported and formed a part of 'MuktiVahini'. The BSF had played an important role in the liberation of Bangladesh.

It has a strength of 2,50,000 personnel in 186 battalions. Some battalions of BSF are also deployed with CRPF in Naxal affected region of Dandakaranya and Jammu and Kashmir. The air wing of the BSF also played a constructive role in the relief work in Uttarakhand during the Kedarnath disaster in 2013.

Two battalions of the BSF, located at Kolkata and Guwahati, are designated as the National Disaster Response Force (NDRF).

Role of BSF During Peacetime

During peacetime, the BSF is associated with the following:

- To promote sense of security among the people living in the border areas
- To prevent trans-border crimes, unauthorised entry into or exit from the territory of India
- To prevent smuggling and any other illegal activities on the border
- Anti-infiltration duties
- To collect trans-border intelligence

Role of BSF in Times of War

During the war, BSF is responsible for:

- Holding ground in assigned sectors
- Limited aggressive action against Central Armed Police or irregular forces of the enemy
- Maintenance of law and order in enemy territory administered under the Army's control
- Guarding of prisoners of war camps
- Acting as guides to the army in border areas
- Assistance in control of refugees
- Provision of escorts
- Performing special tasks connected with intelligence, including raids

➤ 11.1.2 Central Reserve Police Force (CRPF)

The CRPF is the largest Central Armed Police Force in the country. It came into existence as the Crown Representative's Police on 27th July 1939. After India's independence, it became the Central Reserve Police and since then, the Force has achieved remarkable growth in strength and capabilities. It has strength of 234 battalions (Bns) including raising and under-raising Bns. At present, CRPF has 195 executive Bns, 02 Disaster Management Bns, 04 Mahila Bns, 10 RAF Bns, 05 Signal Bns, 10 Commando Bns for Resolute Action (COBRA Bns), 01 Special Duty Group, 01 Parliament Duty Group (PDG) and 40 Group Centres and other allied institutions and training centres. CRPF has also raised 03 NDRF Battalions to assist during natural calamities and disasters. It functions under the aegis of Ministry of Home Affairs (MHA) of the Government of India. The CRPF is headed by an IPS Officer.

Role The CRPF's primary role lies in assisting the State/Union Territories in police operations to maintain law and order contain insurgency and carry out anti Naxal operations. The CRPF also plays an important role in conducting elections across the country. Besides, it also performs guard duties at some of the vital installations and buildings, including the shrine of Mata Vaishno Devi in Jammu, and other religious shrines.

Some specialized formations of CRPF are as follows:

1. **The Rapid Action Force (RAF): It is** a specialised 10 battalion wing of CRPF. It was formed in October 1992, to deal with communal riots and related civil unrest. It is a specialized force with multi-ethnic composition and better mobility for swift action to control communal riots.
2. **Commando Battalions for Resolute Action (COBRA) Bn** : There are 10 specialised battalions named COBRA and these battalions became operational during 2008-09. They are trained and equipped for commando operations especially against Left Wing Extremism and are capable of undertaking intelligence based quick operations.
3. **Special Duty Group (SDG) and Parliament Duty Group (PDG)** : SDG is an elite CRPF unit tasked to provide armed protection to SPG protected places. It comprises of personnel drawn from various units of CRPF. SDG members are trained in combating nuclear and bio-chemical attacks, rescue operations and behavioural management. PDG is also an elite CRPF unit tasked to provide armed protection to Parliament House. The creation of the PDG was mooted in the aftermath of the 2001 Parliament terror attack. It comprises 1,540 personnel drawn from various units of CRPF. PDG members are trained in combating nuclear and bio-chemical attacks, rescue operations and behavioural management. The PDG has distinct units of security personnel, communications experts, quick reaction teams and medical staff.

➤ 11.1.3 Indo-Tibetan Border Police (ITBP)

The ITBP (Indo-Tibetan Border Police) is a border guarding force. ITBP is headed by an IPS officer and is under the administrative control of the Ministry of Home Affairs (MHA). ITBP was established on October 24, 1962 for security along India's border with the Tibet Autonomous Region of China. It was raised with 4 service Batallions in the wake of Indo-China conflict in 1962. Presently, battalions of ITBP are deployed on border guarding duties from Karakoram

Pass in Ladakh to Diphu La in Arunachal Pradesh, covering 3,488 km of the Indo-China Border. Manned border posts are at altitudes as high as 21,000 feet in the western, middle and eastern sectors of the border. ITBP is a mountain trained force and most of the officers and men are professionally trained mountaineers and skiers.

ITBP is a multi-dimensional force with primarily five functions:

- Vigil on the northern borders, detection and prevention of border violations and promotion of the sense of security among the local populace
- Check illegal immigration and trans-border smuggling
- Provide security to sensitive installations and threatened VIPs
- Restore and preserve order in any area in the event of disturbance
- To maintain the peace in the country.

The border posts manned by ITBP are exposed to high velocity storms, snow blizzards, avalanches and landslides, besides the hazards of high altitude and extreme cold, where temperature dips up to minus 40 degrees Celsius.

The ITBP has recently taken on disaster management role. Being the first responder for natural disaster in the Himalayas, the ITBP was the first to establish 06 (now 08) Regional Response Centres in Himachal Pradesh, Uttaranchal and the North-east. It has carried out numerous rescue and relief operations in various disaster situations, which took place in their areas of responsibility as well as other parts of the country. ITBP has already trained 1,032 personnel in disaster management including 98 personnel in radiological and chemical and biological emergencies.

ITBP commando units also provide security to the embassy and consulates of India in Afghanistan. The force has also been providing security to pilgrims during the annual Kailash Mansarovar Yatra since 1981. ITBP provides communication, security and medical cover to the yatris.

ITBP, being deployed in mountains, has developed the expertise in rescue and relief operations in the mountains, which entails specialised skills of very high standard. It is always first in extending rescue and relief in case of natural calamities. It BP played a critical role in the relief operation in Uttarakhand in 2013 ITBP conducts a large number of civic action programmes in remote border and terrorist affected areas to provide free and expert medical, health and hygiene care to the civilian population in remote villages.

➤ 11.1.4 Central Industrial Security Force (CISF)

The CISF (Central Industrial Security Force) provides security cover to 300 industrial units and other establishments located all over India. It was raised in the year 1969. It provides security cover to 307 industrial unit including 59 domestic and international airports and fire protection cover to 86 industrial undertakings. Industrial sectors like atomic power plants, space installations, mints, oil fields and refineries, major ports, the Delhi metro, heavy engineering and steel plants, barrages, fertilizer units, airports and hydroelectric/thermal power plants owned and controlled by the Central PSUs, and currency note presses producing Indian currency are protected by the CISF. In a span of four decades, the force has grown manifold and has a sanctioned strength of 1,33,762 as on 31.12.2012. CISF is headed by an IPS officer and is under the administrative control of Ministry of Home Affairs (MHA). With the globalisation and liberalisation of the economy, CISF has become a premier multi-skilled security agency of the country mandated to provide security to major critical infrastructure installations of the country in diverse regions including terrorist and Naxal affected areas.

The Indian Parliament on February 25, 2009 authorised the provision of Central Industrial Security Force to provide security to private and cooperative establishments across the country for a fee with the passage of the CISF (Amendment) Act, 2008. The Act also provides for deployment of CISF to protect Indian missions abroad and its participation in the UN peacekeeping operations.

The CISF started providing security to the Infosys Bangalore campus in 2009. Infosys Mysore, Reliance Refinery, Jamnagar and the Delhi Metro Airport Express Line are the latest additions to the list of private sector establishments to be placed under CISF cover.

➤ 11.1.5 Sashastra Seema Bal(SSB)

The SSB (Sashastra Seema Bal) is a border guarding Force. SSB is headed by an IPS officer and is under the administrative control of Ministry of Home Affairs (MHA). Its primary role is to guard India's international border with Nepal and Bhutan. It was formerly known as the Special Service Bureau.

SSB (Special Service Bureau) was set up in early 1963 in the wake of the Sino-Indian War. The primary tasks of the force were to provide armed support for RAW (Research and Analysis Wing) and to inculcate feelings of national belonging in the border population and develop their capabilities for resistance through a continuous process of motivation, training, development, welfare programmes and activities in the then NEFA, North Assam(northern areas of Assam state), North Bengal (northern areas of West Bengal state), hills of Uttar Pradesh, Himachal Pradesh and Ladakh.

SSB was renamed as 'Sashastra Seema Bal' in accordance with its new role and came under the administrative control of the Ministry of Home Affairs in the year 2001. This was done after the Kargil War when 'one border one force' concept was adopted. SSB was assigned the duty of manning the 1,751 km long Indo-Nepal Border in 2001. In March 2004, SSB was assigned the task of guarding the 699 km stretch of Indo-Bhutan border along the states of Sikkim, West Bengal, Assam and Arunachal Pradesh. SSB is also the first border guarding force which has decided to recruit women battalions.

SSB is also engaged in counter-insurgency operations in Jammu and Kashmir and anti-naxal operations in Jharkhand and Bihar. It is also performing internal security duties, i.e. election duties and law and order duties, in different parts of India.

The role of SSB comprises the following:

- To promote sense of security among the people living in the border areas
- To prevent trans-border crimes and unauthorised entry or exit from the territory of India
- To prevent smuggling and other illegal activities

➤ 11.1.6 National Security Guard (NSG)

The National Security Guard (NSG) is a special force set up in 1984 as a Federal Contingency Deployment Force that has primarily been utilised for counter-terrorism activities and was created by the Cabinet Secretariat under the National Security Guard Act of the Indian Parliament in 1986. It works completely within the Central Armed Police Forces structure. NSG is a 100% deputation force and all personnel posted are on deputation from Army, CAPs, State police and other organisation. Its primary task is to engage and neutralise terrorist threats in specific situations and undertake counter hijack and hostage rescue missions. They are also assigned the task of providing mobile security protection to VVIPs. The NSG is an elite force providing a second line of defence to the nation. They have played a pivotal role in safeguarding the unity of India and have commendably foiled attempts of anti-national elements to tear apart the social fabric of the country. The NSG has maintained an edge over terrorist outfits in the possession of latest technology. They are considered among the best special operations units in the world. NSG is headed by an IPS Officer and is under the administrative control of the Ministry of Home Affairs (MHA).

The NSG's specific goals include:

- Neutralisation of terrorist threats
- Handling hijacking situations in air and on land
- Bomb disposal (search, detection and neutralisation of IEDs)
- Engaging and neutralising terrorists in specific situations
- Hostage rescue

NSG performed *Operation Black Tornado* and *Operation Cyclone* to flush out terrorists and rescue hostages after multiple attacks across Mumbai in the 26/11 attack in 2008. Four new NSG hubs were established in Mumbai, Hyderabad, Chennai and Kolkata after this incident.

The National Bomb Data Centre (NBBC) under NSG maintains the National Bomb Data Centre at Maneswar and conducts post blast studies in various parts of the country mostly on request from State authorities. It maintains a data bank on explosives and incidents of blasts which may be of use to security forces.

➤ 11.1.7 Special Protection Group (SPG)

The Special Protection Group (SPG) is the executive protection agency of the Government of India. It is responsible for the protection of the Prime Minister of India, former Prime Ministers and their immediate family members. The Force is under the control of the Cabinet Secretariat.

The force was established in 1985 after the assassination of Mrs Indira Gandhi, erstwhile Prime Minister. It provides proximate security to the protected, including protection provided from close quarters, journey on foot, road, rail, aircraft, watercraft or any other means of transport, and includes places of functions, engagements, residence, etc. They comprise of ring round teams, isolation cordons, the sterile zone, and the rostrum and access control to the person or members of his immediate family.

➤ 11.1.8 Railway Protection Force (RPF)

The Railway Protection Force (RPF) of the Indian Railways is entrusted with the task of protecting the lifeline of the country namely the Indian Railways. The strength of RPF is about 65,000.

The duties of the Railway Protection Force include:

- To engage in all conducive means for the free movement of the railways
- Protection and safeguarding of railway property
- Protection and safeguarding of passengers, their belongings and passenger areas

Originally the force was called Watch & Ward and it functioned under the administrative control of railway administration. Later on, this force was renamed as Railway Protection Force and its members were provided with the power to arrest without warrant for the unlawful possession of railway property. The term railway property included only the properties owned by the railway administration. In due course of time, the definition for the term Railway Property was extended and it included the properties owned by, or in the charge of or entrusted with the railways. The offenders are booked under the Railway Property (Unlawful Possession) Act 1966 which is shortly known as RP (UP) Act 1966. Now the Railway Protection Force has a separate administrative system and functions under the general supervision of the Railway Administration.

➤ 11.2 Central Paramilitary Forces (CPMFs)

Central Para Military Forces (CPMFs) Assam Rifles and Indian Coast Guard are the main CPMFs after reclassification.

Assam Rifles Assam Rifles is fondly known as 'Friends of the North East People'. It is the oldest Para Military Force in the Country with its Headquarter at Shillong. The Force is completely deployed in the North East and is mandated for dual role of maintaining internal security in the North East and guarding the Indo-Myanmar border. It is led and head by Army officers. It assists Indian armed forces but reports to MHA. It is under administrative control of MHA but operates under Army.

Indian Coast Guard Its mission is the protection of India's maritime interests and enforcement of maritime law; with jurisdiction over the territorial waters of India, including its contiguous zone and exclusive economic zone. It operates under the Ministry of Defence. After the 2008 Mumbai attacks, the government initiated a program to expand the ICG force, assets and infrastructure. The force is expected to be tripled between 2010 and 2019 in manpower, vessels and aircraft.

11.3 Security Agencies and their Mandates

11.3.1 Intelligence Bureau (IB)

The Intelligence Bureau (IB) is India's internal intelligence agency and reputedly the world's oldest intelligence agency. It was recast as the Central Intelligence Bureau in 1947 under the Ministry of Home Affairs.

Serving since December 2012, Syed Asif Ibrahim is the current director of the IB.

The Bureau comprises employees from law enforcement agencies, mostly from the Indian Police Service (IPS) and the military. However, the Director of Intelligence Bureau (DIB) has always been an IPS officer. In addition to domestic intelligence responsibilities, the IB is particularly entrusted with intelligence collection in border areas, following the 1951 recommendations of the Himmatsinhji Committee (also known as the North and North-east Border Committee). Prior to 1947, this task was entrusted to military intelligence organisations. All spheres of human activity within India and in the neighbourhood are allocated to the charter of duties of the Intelligence Bureau. The IB is used to garner intelligence from within India and also execute counter-intelligence and counter-terrorism tasks.

The Intelligence Bureau reportedly has a lot of successes to its credit, but operations conducted by the IB are rarely declassified. Due to the extreme secrecy surrounding the agency, there is little concrete information available about it or its activities.

The IB was initially India's internal and external intelligence agency. After the Sino-Indian War of 1962, and later on, India-Pakistan War in 1965, it was bifurcated in 1968 and entrusted with the task of internal intelligence only.

IB is the main coordinating agency regarding counter-terrorism. It coordinates with various states' police all over the country.

The IB has had mixed success in counter-terrorism. It was reported in 2008 that the IB had been successful in busting terror modules. It alerted the police before the Hyderabad blasts and gave repeated warnings of a possible attack on Mumbai through the sea before the November 2008 Mumbai attacks.

11.3.2 National Investigation Agency (NIA)

The National Investigation Agency (NIA) is a federal agency established by the Indian government to combat terror in India. It acts as the central counter-terrorism law enforcement agency. The agency is empowered to deal with terror related crimes across states without special permission from the states. The Agency came into existence with the enactment of the National Investigation Agency Act 2008 by the Parliament on December 31, 2008.

NIA was created after the 2008 Mumbai terror attacks as the need for a central agency to combat terrorism were realised. The founding Director-General of NIA was Radha Vinod Raju, and he served till January 31, 2010. He was succeeded by Sharad Chandra Sinhatill March 2013 when he was appointed the member of the National Human Rights Commission of India. In July 2013, Sharad Kumar was appointed as the Chief of NIA.

The Agency has been empowered to conduct investigation and prosecution of offenses under the Acts specified in the Schedule of the NIA Act. A State Government may request the Central Government to hand over the investigation of a case to the NIA, provided the case has been registered for the offenses as contained in the schedule to the NIA Act. Central Government can also order NIA to take over investigation of any scheduled offense anywhere in India. Officers of the NIA who are drawn from the Indian Police Service and the Indian Revenue Service have all powers, privileges and liabilities which the police officers have in connection with investigation of any offense. In recent times, the NIA has had big successes in busting an IM module and arresting its key functionaries.

Multi Agency Centre (MAC)

MAC is a multi-agency centre for counter-terrorism whose mandate is to share terrorism related inputs on a day-to-day basis.

Multi Agency Centre (MAC) was created at Delhi and Subsidiary Multi Agency Centres (SMACs) in various states comprising representatives from various security agencies, for streamlining intelligence efforts. Later, the Union Home Minister reviewed the security situation and issued Multi Agency Centre (functions, powers and duties) Order, 2008 on December 31, 2008. MAC-SMAC is functioning since 2002 and has been reoperationalised with effect from 2009. As a follow up of the above order, 24x7 Control Rooms have been set up at Multi Agency Centre (MAC) at New Delhi and the Subsidiary Multi Agency Centres (SMACs) at State Level and at Headquarters of Intelligence Wings of other agencies to ensure timely sharing of information and better co-ordination between intelligence agencies. Daily meetings of Nodal Officers of 25 member agencies are being conducted on every working day. Presently, MAC-SMAC network has 416 nodes spread across the country and connected to MAC HQ at New Delhi. This includes 31 SMAC HQs and 32 SSBs located at State Capitals (More details on MAC is given in Chapter 2).

National Intelligence Grid (NATGRID)

The National Intelligence Grid or NATGRID is an integrated intelligence grid that will link the databases of several departments and ministries of the Government of India so as to collect comprehensive patterns of intelligence that can be readily accessed by intelligence agencies. It was first proposed in the aftermath of the terrorist attacks on Mumbai in 2008 and was to be operational in 2013 but is yet to happen.

NATGRID is an intelligence sharing network that collates data from the standalone databases of various agencies and ministries of the Indian government. It is a counter-terrorism measure that collects and collates a host of information from government databases, including tax and bank account details, credit card transactions, visa and immigration records and itineraries of rail and air travel. This combined data will be made available to 11 central agencies-Research and Analysis Wing, the Intelligence Bureau, Central Bureau of Investigation, Financial Intelligence Unit, Central Board of Direct Taxes, Directorate of Revenue Intelligence, Enforcement Directorate, Narcotics Control Bureau, Central Board of Excise and Customs and the Directorate General of Central Excise Intelligence.

Unlike the NCTC and the NIA which are central organisations, the NATGRID is essentially a tool that will enable security agencies to locate and obtain relevant information on terror suspects from pooled data of various organisations and services in the country. It will help identify, capture and prosecute terrorists and help pre-empt terrorist plots.

PROBABLE QUESTIONS BASED ON THIS CHAPTER

1. What do you understand by Central Armed Police Force?
2. What is the mandate of the National Investigation Agency (NIA)?
3. What is the role of MAC and NATGRID in strengthening internal security?

CHAPTER

12

Disaster Management

12.1 Definition of Disaster

India is one of the most disaster-prone countries in the world. Its location and geographical features render it vulnerable to a number of natural hazards including cyclones, droughts, floods, earthquakes, forest fires, landslides and avalanches. A disaster is an event that causes sudden disruption to normal life of a society and causes damage to property and lives, to such an extent that normal social and economic mechanisms available to the society are inadequate to restore normalcy.

According to the United Nations, *'Disaster is a serious disruption of the functioning of a community or a society involving widespread human, material, economic or environmental losses and impacts, which exceeds the ability of the affected community or society to cope using its own resources'*.

It is the result of a combination of a number of factors which include:

- Exposure to natural hazards
- Existing conditions of vulnerability
- Insufficient capacity or measures to cope with potential negative consequences
- Inappropriate management of risks and vulnerabilities

A hazard is a threat, a future source of danger with the potential to cause damage to:

- People: Death, injury, disease and stress
- Property: Damage to property, economic loss, loss of livelihood and status
- Environment: Loss of fauna and flora, pollution, loss of bio-diversity

12.2 Types of Disasters

Disasters can be classified into two types:

- Natural disasters
- Man-made disasters

12.2.1 Natural Disasters

Natural disasters are caused by:

- Floods
- Earthquake
- Tsunami
- Drought
- Cyclone
- Landslide
- Avalanche
- Hurricane
- Volcano eruption
- Cold wave
- Forest Fire

12.2.2 Man-made Disasters

Man-made disasters can be classified as:

- Nuclear disasters
- Chemical disasters
- Biological disasters
- Pandemic emergencies, epidemic
- Fire (Building, coal, forest, oil)
- Pollution (Air, water, industrial)
- Deforestation
- Accidents (Road, rail, sea, air)
- Industrial accidents
- Riots
- Hijacking
- Terrorism

12.3 Phases of Disaster Management

12.3.1 Phase 1: Before the Crisis

Preparedness: This is the period when the potential hazard, risk and vulnerabilities can be assessed and steps can be taken for:

1. Preventing and mitigating the crisis, and
2. Preparing for actual occurrence.

Crisis can also be mitigated through various short term measures which either reduce the scale and intensity of the threat or improve the durability and capacity of the elements at risk. For example, better enforcement of building codes and zoning regulations, proper maintenance of drainage systems, better awareness and public education to reduce the risks of hazards, etc. help in containing the damage.

➤ 12.3.2 Phase 2: During the Crisis

Emergency Response: When a crisis actually occurs, those affected by it require a speedy response to alleviate and minimise suffering and losses. In this phase, certain 'primary activities' become indispensable. These are:

1. Evacuation
2. Search and rescue, followed by
3. Provision of basic needs, such as food, clothing, shelter, medicines and other necessities essential for bringing bring the life of the affected community back to a degree of normalcy

➤ 12.3.3 Phase 3: Post Crisis

1. *Recovery:* This is the stage when efforts are made to achieve early recovery and reduce vulnerability and future risks. It comprises activities that encompass two overlapping phases of rehabilitation and reconstruction.
2. *Rehabilitation:* Includes provision of temporary public utilities and housing as interim measures to assist long term recovery.
3. *Reconstruction:* Includes construction of damaged infrastructure and habitats and enabling sustainable livelihoods.

➤ 12.4 Elements of Disaster Management

We have described above the three phases of disaster management. Figure 12.1 describes the various aspects of the three phases.

➤ 12.4.1 Risk Reduction

Disaster risk reduction strategies have the potential to save thousands of lives by the adoption of simple preventive measures. Lack of coherent disaster reduction strategies and the absence of a 'culture of prevention' are the major causes for increasing casualties due to disasters. Disaster risk reduction (disaster reduction) has been defined as the 'systematic development and application of policies, strategies and practices to minimise vulnerabilities, hazards and the unfolding of disaster impacts throughout a society, in the broad context of sustainable development'.

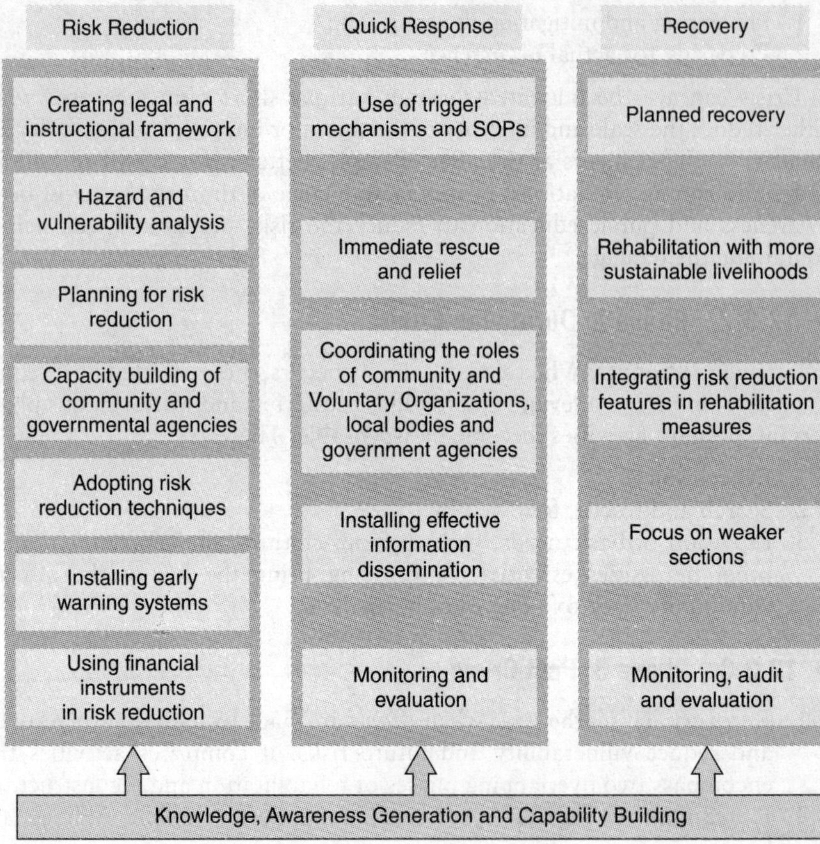

Fig. 12.1 *Elements of Disaster Management*

Disaster reduction strategies include appraisal of likelihood and intensity of hazards and analysis of vulnerabilities thereof to the community. Building of institutional capabilities and community preparedness is the next step. Crucial to all these efforts, however, is the existence of a 'safety culture' in societies. Inputs like education, training and capacity building play a very significant role. It needs to be understood that such preparedness cannot be a 'one time' effort, but is a continuous process.

Knowledge plays an important role in disaster reduction. The traditional knowledge available with the community has to be used along with knowledge acquired through research and past experiences.

The disaster risk reduction framework is composed of the following fields of action:

1. Policies towards risk management
2. Assessment of risk, including hazard analysis and vulnerability
3. Generating risk awareness with the help of mass media and social media
4. Preparation of plans for risk mitigation
5. Implementation of the plan

6. Early warning systems with the help of latest technology relating to data capture transmission, analysis and even dissemination
7. Use of knowledge
8. Information: Effective disaster risk management depends on the informed participation of all stakeholders. The exchange of information and easily accessible communication practices play key roles. Data is crucial for ongoing research, national planning, monitoring hazards and assessing risks. The widespread and consistent availability of current and accurate data is fundamental to all aspects of disaster risk reduction.

Mitigation

Mitigation involves:

- Measures aimed at reducing the impact of disasters
- Efforts to prevent hazards from developing into disasters altogether
- Differs from the other phases because it focuses on long-term measures for reducing or eliminating risk
- It embraces actions taken in advance of a disaster to reduce its effects on a community

Significance of Mitigation A number of special programmes are in operation for mitigating the impact of natural disasters and local communities have developed their own indigenous coping mechanisms. In the event of an emergency, the mobilisation of community action supported by NGOs add strength to the national disaster management capacity.

Despite initiating various disaster mitigation measures, there has been little improvement. Accordingly, India has taken initiatives for linking disaster mitigation with development plans, promoting the application of effective communication systems and information technology, insurance, extensive public awareness and education campaigns (particularly in rural areas), involving the private sector and strengthening institutional mechanisms and international community cooperation.

➤ 12.4.2 Quick Response

Quick response can save lives, protect property and lessen disruptions caused by crises. This calls for a total and effective response, which must subsume the coordinated response of the entire governmental system as also the civil society. The response should not only incorporate traditional coping mechanisms, which have evolved over the centuries but also involve meticulous planning and coordination. Cumulative experience with crisis management over the years points to an urgent need for putting in place a holistic and effective response mechanism which is professional, result-oriented, innovative and people-centric. Quick response entails the following:

- This phase includes mobilisation of necessary emergency services and first responders in the disaster area. This is likely to include a first wave of core emergency services, such as fire-fighters, police and ambulance crews. They may be supported by a number of secondary emergency services, such as specialist rescue teams.

- It entails restoring physical facilities, rehabilitation of affected families/populations, restoration of lost livelihoods and reconstruction efforts.
- Retrospectively, it brings to light the flaws in Policy and Planning with respect to infrastructure, its location, social scheme, etc.

Significance

The significance of quick response can be stated as under:

- It has immediate mitigation impact and losses can be minimised to a greater degree. According to the estimate of the insurance industry, natural disasters represent 85% insured catastrophe.
- Thousands of lives lost and millions of people are left weakened each year due to reluctance on part of donors to invest in measures that reduce the impact of disasters. (*World Disaster Report 2002*)
- Long term resilience of vulnerable communities

Issues

The issues involved are:

- Coordination among the concerned actors involved (government, civil society and international donor organisation). Recent example is the case of Uttarakhand floods (June 2013) where international organisations found it hard to immediately get government approval to start work.
- Institutionalisation of disaster response structure at local level.

➤ 12.4.3 Recovery

Recovery is an important phase which involves:

- In the long-term aftermath of a disaster, when restoration efforts are in addition to regular services, it involves implementation of actions to promote sustainable redevelopment (reconstruction, rehabilitation).
- It differs from the response phase in its focus; recovery efforts are concerned with issues and decisions that must be made after immediate needs are addressed. Recovery efforts are primarily concerned with actions that involve rebuilding destroyed property, re-employment, and the repair of other essential infrastructure.
- The recovery phase starts when the immediate threat to human life has subsided. In the reconstruction, it is desirable to reconsider the location or construction material of the property.
- Community resilience is a key factor in disaster recovery.
- This phase encompasses three overlapping phases of 3Rs

  Relief: It is the period immediately after the disaster when steps are taken to meet the need of survivors.

  Rehabilitation: These are activities undertaken to support the victims' return to normalcy and reintegration in regular community function.

It encompasses provision of temporary employment and restoration of livelihood.

Reconstruction: It is an attempt to return communities to improved pre-disaster functioning.

12.5 Disaster Response in India

Over the centuries, local communities have developed their own indigenous survival mechanisms. This rich storehouse of knowledge is a part of our country's legacy. The *Arthashastra* (a treatise on public administration by Chanakya in the 4th century BC), devoted a section to mitigation measures to combat famines. The community is usually the first responder in case of a disaster. Field level response on behalf of the government in rural areas is provided by the nearest police station and the revenue functionary (patwari/patel/talati/karnam etc); in urban areas the response is articulated by agencies like the civic authorities, the fire brigade and the local police station. At present, panchayats do not have the capacity to react institutionally in any effective manner to such situations and it is the district administration which retains the basic responsibility of handling crises situations, with the Collector playing a pivotal role.

India is fraught with challenges and unique opportunities for low cost, disaster mitigation interventions that would add value to the existing work carried out by government organisations, NGOs and donors. Devolution and decentralisation have created new challenges for the sector, generating renewed scope for action at the grass-roots level where disaster preparedness and planning decisions are most effective. There is a vast pool of experienced organisational, technical and scientific resources and disaster related information and knowledge within the region.

India has integrated administrative machinery for disaster management at the National, State, District and Sub-District levels. The Central Government supplements the State relief efforts by initiating supportive action. An elaborate procedural mechanism and the allocation of resources to facilitate emergency management operations is outlined in relief manuals and codes backed by the Contingency Action Plan (CAP). The CAP facilitates the relief operations, procedures and focal roles of central ministries and departments. The Crisis Management Group headed by the Cabinet Secretary and consisting of nodal ministries (particularly the Ministry of Home Affairs and Agriculture) oversee response coordination, carry out an assessment and make recommendations for assistance.

State Governments have the responsibility for undertaking rescue and relief measures in the event of a natural calamity through the State Relief Commissioner, Relief and Rehabilitation Department or the Department of Revenue. District Coordination and Review Committee headed by the Collector involves the participation of related agencies, departments and NGOs.

➤ 12.5.1 Legal Framework

The Government enacted the National Disaster Management Act (NDMA) 2005 on December 26, 2005 to provide for institutional mechanism for drawing up and monitoring the implementation of disaster management plans, ensuring measures by various wings of the government for preventing and mitigating effects of disaster and for undertaking a holistic, coordinated and prompt response to any disaster situation. The Act provides for setting up of a National Disaster Management Authority (NDMA) under the chairmanship of the Prime Minister, State Disaster Management Authorities (SDMAs) under the chairmanship of Chief Ministers and District Disaster Management Authorities (DDMAs) under the chairmanship of District Magistrates. The Act further provides for constitution of National Executive Committee (NEC), National Institute of Disaster Management (NIDM) and National Disaster Response Force (NDRF). It also provides for the concerned ministries and departments to draw up department-wise plans in accordance with the National Disaster Management Plan. In addition, the Act contains provision for constitution of National Disaster Response Fund and National Disaster Mitigation Fund and similar funds at the state and the district levels. The Act also provides for specific roles to local bodies, including Panchayati Raj Institutions (PRIs) and Urban Local Bodies (ULBs) in disaster management. The NDMA, NEC and NIDM have since been constituted in accordance with the provisions of the Act to discharge the powers and functions envisaged for them under the Act.

At the district level, the DM Act 2005 provides for the constitution of District Disaster Management Authorities under the chairmanship of the District Magistrate/ Collector while the elected representative of the local authority would be the co-chairperson. In those districts where Zilla Parishads exist, the chairman would be the ex-officio co-chairperson of the District Disaster Management Authority. The district authority shall act as the planning, coordinating and implementing body for disaster management in the district and take all measures for the purposes of disaster management in the district in accordance with the guidelines laid down by the national and state authorities.

The concept of disaster management plan at different levels has received a new orientation with the passage of the National Disaster Management Act. Earlier such plans were being prepared at the district level only. Under the UNDP-DRM programme, such plans are being prepared at the village level as well.

The planning process has been carried down to the sub-divisional, block and village levels. Each village in multi-hazard prone district will have a Disaster Management Plan. The Disaster Management Committee which draws up the plans consists of elected representatives at the village level, local authorities, government functionaries, including doctors/paramedics of primary health centres located in the village, primary school teachers, etc. The plan encompasses prevention, mitigation and preparedness measures. The Disaster Management Teams at the village level will consist of members of youth organisations like Nehru Yuvak Kendra and other non-governmental organisations as well as able bodied volunteers from the village. The teams are provided basic training in evacuation, search and rescue, first aid trauma counselling, etc. The disaster management committee will review the disaster management plan at least once in a year. It would also generate awareness among the people in the village about the dos and don'ts for specific hazards depending on the vulnerability of the village. A large number of village level disaster management committees and disaster management teams have already been constituted.

Long-term planning and preparedness for disaster mitigation form the process of planned development in India. Science and technology inputs constitute its basic thrust, manifested in development of forecasting and warning systems, disaster resistant construction technologies and appropriate cropping systems. India has elaborate cyclone detection and tracking systems, flood forecasting and warning systems.

➤ 12.5.2 National Disaster Management Act, 2005

The Act encompasses the following:

1. The Act calls for the establishment of National Disaster Management Authority (NDMA), with the Prime Minister of India as chairperson.
2. The Act under Section 8 enjoins the Central Government to constitute a National Executive Committee (NEC) to assist the National Authority. The NEC is composed of Secretary level officers of the Government of India in the Ministries of Home, Agriculture, Atomic Energy, Defence, Drinking Water Supply, Environment and Forests, Finance (expenditure), Health, Power, Rural Development, Science and Technology, Space, Telecommunications, Urban Development and Water Resources, with the Home Secretary serving as the Chairperson, ex-officio. The Chief of the Integrated Defence Staff of the Chiefs of Staff Committee is an ex-officio member of the NEC. The NEC is responsible for the preparation of the National Disaster Management Plan for the whole country and to ensure that it is 'reviewed and updated annually'.
3. All State Governments are mandated under Section 14 of the Act to establish a State Disaster Management Authority (SDMA). The SDMA consists of the Chief Minister of the State, who is the Chairperson, and no more than eight members appointed by the Chief Minister. State Executive Committee is responsible for drawing up the state disaster management plan and implementing the National Plan. The SDMA is mandated to ensure that all the departments of the State prepare disaster management plans as prescribed by the national and state authorities.
4. The Act directs to establish District Disaster Management Authority (DDMA). The Chairperson of DDMA will be the Collector or the District Magistrate or the Deputy Commissioner of the district. The elected representative of the area is member of the DDMA as an ex-officio Chairperson.
5. The Act provides for constituting a National Disaster Response Force 'for the purpose of specialist response to a threatening disaster situation

or disaster' under the Director General to be appointed by the Central Government.

The implementation of the National Disaster Management Act 2005 has been slow, and slack. In 2013, the Supreme Court, in response to a PIL, issued notices to the Governments of Uttarakhand, Tamil Nadu, Orissa, Andhra Pradesh, Gujarat, Rajasthan, Maharashtra and the Central Government for alleged failure to implement the National Disaster Management Act 2005.

The Act has been criticised for marginalising non-governmental organisations (NGOs), elected local representatives, local communities and civic groups; and for fostering a hierarchical, bureaucratic, command and control, 'top down' approach that gives the central, state and district authorities sweeping powers.

12.6 Institutions for Disaster Management

12.6.1 National Disaster Management Authority (NDMA)

The National Disaster Management Authority (NDMA) is an independent, autonomous and constitutionally-established disaster preparedness federal institution and is responsible to deal with the whole spectrum of disaster management and preparedness in the country.

The NDMA formulates and enforces national disaster policies at federal and provisional levels and collaborates closely with various government ministries, military forces and United Nations based organisations to jointly coordinate efforts to conduct disaster management, search and rescue, and a wide range of humanitarian operations in the country and abroad. The NDMA aims to develop sustainable operational capacity and professional competence to undertake its humanitarian operations at its full capacity.

NDMA has been constituted with the Prime Minister of India as its Chairman, a Vice-Chairman with the status of Cabinet Minister, and eight members with the status of Ministers of State. Each of the members has a well-defined functional domain covering various states as also disaster specific areas of focus and concern. To carry out the mandated functions, NDMA has evolved a lean and professional organisation which is IT-enabled and knowledge-based. Skills and expertise of the specialists are extensively used to address all disaster related issues. A functional and operational infrastructure has been built which is appropriate for disaster management involving uncertainties coupled with desired plans of action.

NDMA, as the apex body, is mandated to lay down the policies, plans and guidelines for disaster management to ensure timely and effective response to disasters. Towards this, it has the following responsibilities:

- Lay down policies on disaster management
- Approve the National Plan
- Approve plans prepared by the Ministries or Departments of the Government of India in accordance with the National Plan
- Lay down guidelines to be followed by the State Authorities in drawing up the State Plan

- Lay down guidelines to be followed by the different Ministries or Departments of the Government of India for the purpose of integrating the measures for prevention of disaster, or the mitigation of its effects in their development plans and projects
- Coordinate the enforcement and implementation of the policy and plan for disaster management
- Recommend provision of funds for the purpose of mitigation
- Provide such support to other countries affected by major disasters as may be determined by the Central Government
- Take such other measures for the prevention of disaster, or the mitigation, or preparedness and capacity building for dealing with the threatening disaster situations or disasters as it may consider necessary
- Lay down broad policies and guidelines for the functioning of the National Institute of Disaster Management

➤ 12.6.2 The National Institute of Disaster Management (NIDM)

The NIDM was constituted under the Disaster Management Act 2005. The National Institute of Disaster Management (NIDM) is a premier national organisation working for human resource development at the national level in the area of disaster mitigation and management. It is an autonomous body under the Ministry of Home Affairs. It has been entrusted with the nodal national responsibility for human resource development, capacity building, training, research, documentation and policy advocacy in the field of disaster management. Its objectives are:

(i) To undertake quality research
(ii) To work as a national resource centre
(iii) To professionalise disaster management
(iv) To promote training
(v) To build partnerships with stakeholders and other institutions
(vi) To link learning and action

➤ 12.7 Role of Various Governments and Other Agencies in Disaster Management

➤ 12.7.1 Role of the Union Government

Although the State Government concerned has the primary responsibility for crisis management, the Union Government plays a key supportive role in terms of physical and financial resources and providing complementary measures, such as early warning and co-ordination of efforts of all union ministries, departments and organisations. At the apex level, a Cabinet Committee on Natural Calamities reviews the crisis situation. A high level committee of ministers under the chairmanship of Minister of Agriculture deals with the issue of financial support to be provided to the State Governments from the National Disaster Response Fund, if the funds available with the State

Governments under State Disaster Response Fund are not adequate. Matters relating to nuclear, biological and chemical emergencies are looked after by the Cabinet Committee on Security.

➤ 12.7.2 National Crisis Management Committee

The Cabinet Secretary, as the highest executive officer, heads the National Crisis Management Committee (NCMC). Secretaries of ministries and departments concerned and heads of other organisations are members of NCMC, which reviews and monitors crisis situations on a regular basis and gives directions to the Crisis Management Group, as deemed necessary. The NCMC can give directions to any ministry, department or organisation for specific action needed for meeting the crisis situation.

As disaster management is a multi-disciplinary process, all Central Ministries and Departments have a key role in the field of disaster management. In view of the highly technical and specific nature of certain disaster events such as aviation disasters, rail accidents, chemical disasters and biological disasters etc; the ministries dealing with that particular subject have the nodal responsibility for handling that particular type of disaster, as shown-

Nodal Ministries/Department for Disaster Management at the National Level

Droughts	Ministry of Agriculture
Epidemics and Biological Disasters	Ministry of Health
Chemical or Industrial Chemical disasters	Ministry of Environment & Forest
Nuclear Accidents	Department of Atomic Energy
Railway Accidents	Ministry of Railways
Air Accidents	Ministry of Civil Aviation
Natural Disasters except Drought & Epidemics and Civil Strife	Ministry of Home Affairs

The Secretaries of the Nodal Ministries and Departments of GOI, i.e. the Ministry of Home Affairs (MHA), Agriculture, Civil Aviation, Environment and Forests, Health, Atomic Energy, Space, Earth Sciences, Water Resources, Mines, Railways etc. are all members of the NEC and function as nodal agencies for specific disasters based on their core competencies or as assigned to them. The coordination between various nodal ministries / departments is done by National Executive Committee (NEC), which is headed by Home Secretary. The NEC has to prepare the national plan for disaster management based on the National Disaster Management Policy.

➤ 12.7.3 Crisis Management Group

The Crisis Management Group (CMG) consists of nodal officers from various concerned ministries. Apart from CMG, the National Executive Committee headed by the Home Secretary performs the statutory coordination and functions as per the DM Act, 2005

The CMG's functions are to review annual contingency plans formulated by various ministries, departments and organisations in their respective sectors, measures required for dealing with natural disasters, coordinate the activities of the Union Ministries and State Governments in relation to disaster preparedness and relief, and to obtain information from the nodal officers on all these issues. In the event of a disaster, the CMG meets frequently to review relief operations and extends all possible assistance required by the affected states to overcome the situation. The Resident Commissioner of the affected state is also associated with such meetings.

➤ 12.7.4 Funding Mechanism

Each state has a corpus of funds, called State Disaster Response Fund, administered by a state level committee headed by the Chief Secretary of the State Government. The size of the corpus is determined with reference to the expenditure normally incurred by the state on relief and rehabilitation over the past ten years. In case the funds under State Disaster Response Fund are not sufficient to meet the specific requirements, State Governments can seek assistance from the National Disaster Response Fund—a fund created at Central Government level. Both these funds, as the names suggest, are meant for relief and rehabilitation and do not cover either mitigation or reconstruction works, which have to be funded separately by the State or Union Government.

➤ 12.7.5 Role of State Government

In India, the basic responsibility to undertake rescue, relief and rehabilitation measures in the event of natural disasters rests with the state government. Since the very beginning, the entire structure of crisis administration in the state governments had been oriented towards post disaster relief and rehabilitation. Most of the states have Relief Commissioners who are in charge of the relief and rehabilitation measures. Most of the states have switched over to a Disaster Management Department with the required linkages with the various development and regulatory departments concerned with prevention, mitigation and preparedness.

Every state has a Crisis Management Committee under the chairpersonship of the Chief Secretary, consisting of secretaries in charge of concerned departments, which reviews crisis situations on a day-to-day basis at the time of crisis, coordinates the activities of all departments and provides decision support system to the district administration. At the ministers' level, a Cabinet Committee on Natural Calamities under the chairpersonship of the Chief Minister takes stock of situations and is responsible for all important policy decisions.

➤ 12.7.6 Role of District Administration

The District Magistrate/Collector has the responsibility for overall management of disasters in the district. He has the authority to mobilise the response machinery and has been given financial powers to draw money under the provisions of the General Financial Rules/Treasury Codes. All departments of the State Government, including the police, fire services, public works, irrigation etc., work in a coordinated manner under the leadership of the Collector during a disaster, except in metropolitan areas where the municipal body plays a major role. The District Collector also enjoys the authority to request for assistance from the Armed Forces if circumstances so demand. NGOs have also been effective in providing relief, rescue and rehabilitation in recent times.

➤ 12.7.7 Role of Local Self-Governments

Local self-governments, both rural and urban, have emerged as important tiers of governance, after the 73rd and 74th Amendments to the Constitution. For the people, they are also the nearest units of administration and are among the first responders to any crisis besides being closely knit with the communities. These units can thus play an important role in crisis management under the overall leadership of the District Administration.

➤ 12.7.8 Role of Public/NGO/Civil Society/Media

The local community is usually the first responder in case of a disaster. Local community also carries traditional knowledge and relevant counter measures regarding disaster management. So the role of local community must be utilised with the help of NGOs and media. They should be encouraged to play an active role in all three phases of disaster management. District administration should also focus on capacity building, participation and empowerment of these stakeholders in disaster management. Mobilisation of community action supported by local NGOs, along with government machinery is a must for quick, efficient and effective response. For this, healthy coordination must exist between local administration and local community/NGOs. Local NGOs and civil society must work on developing a deep culture of safety and prevention in society.

NGOs, civil society and media also play an active role as pressure groups in a democracy so that any laxity on part of the government can be traced and fixed. So, the public and the NGOs should keep a close vigil over the functioning of the government regarding disaster management and render their services as a watchdog.

➤ 12.8 What is Needed?

We cannot prevent natural hazards, which are endemic to our geology, geography, climate, social and cultural settings, but we can certainly strive to manage crisis more efficiently so that hazards do not degenerate into disasters. With a coherent and meaningful crisis management strategy in place, it is quite possible to visualize our country, despite its manifold hazards, as a place that will eventually be free of all disasters. In the realm of crisis management, announcing a policy, or promulgating a law, or creating an institution is a relatively easy task; the challenge lies in implementing policies to achieve the desired outcomes. Crisis management, a governance issue that is both vital and complex, is at the core of India's administrative system. The system requires innovative thinking and fundamental changes in order to quicken the emergency responses of the administration and increase the effectiveness of the machinery to meet the crisis situation and enhance crisis preparedness. To that end, it is necessary that the apparatus of crisis management should perform and deliver. What is needed is ushering in a new paradigm in the quality and efficacy of our institutional capacity and delivery mechanisms while, at the same time, ensuring that they are embedded in both the structures of authority and the mechanisms of accountability.

Our aim should not only be having more efficient systems of governance but also innovative ways of capacity building and empowerment of all stakeholders at all levels, including panchayats and the community, strategic applications of science and technology, realisation of a sound emergency communication network, building safe homes and infrastructure, and learning from research and development, as also from the experiences of handling crisis situations in the past. Each of these tasks is a challenge and calls for careful strategy of planning and implementation coupled with coordinated efforts of a variety of players, both within and outside the governmental structure. Our target should be establishing the synergy and convergence of advances in the technological and knowledge era with our rich socio-cultural practices and indigenous coping mechanisms. Systematic preparedness, early warning, quick response and sustainable recovery have been the cornerstones of approach to disaster management.

➤ 12.8.1 Institutional Support of Science and Technology Institutions for Disaster Management

Disaster management depends heavily upon the inputs from various science and technology institutions. Indeed, major improvements in disaster management efforts may be attributed to developments in science and technology. As crisis management is multidisciplinary in nature, the relevant research is carried out in several sector-wise research and development organisations. The 2nd Administrative Reforms Committee has recommended that The National Disaster Management Authority, assisted by NIDM, may facilitate a common platform between the science and technology organisations and the users of relevant technologies. Such mechanisms may be made operational both at the Union and State levels.

➤ 12.8.2 Professionalisation of Disaster Management

Institutional development for disaster management in the country has clearly suffered on account of paucity of professionally qualified personnel. While civil servants and other senior personnel in organisations like the police, armed forces and municipal bodies have provided a leadership role and their leadership will continue to be required, it is time that special attention is paid to the long-felt need to professionalise disaster management in the country.

The best practices in disaster management are the strategies and methods perfected by several developed countries and India can take advantage from exposure to these practices. It is, therefore, desirable that the possibility of bilateral agreements with foreign governments for exchange of experiences and learning from their documentation and research efforts be fully explored.

➤ 12.8.3 Use of Mass Media and Social Media

Mass media plays a very important role in spreading awareness about disasters. Immediately after a major disaster in any part of the world, the curiosity and apprehension among the communities about their own risk is at its maximum. This is an opportune time to carry out public awareness campaigns and use media to focus on generating awareness about the risk the community is exposed to. This could best be achieved through a healthy partnership between the media and the disaster management machinery.

An important input in such awareness generation programmes could be the lessons that have been learnt from disasters in the past or from those in other areas. For this purpose, the details of all such disasters need to be properly documented and kept in the public domain. The District Disaster Management Authorities, the State Disaster Management Authorities and the NDMA should have these details along with the lessons learnt, on their respective websites.

➤ 12.8.4 Building Community Resilience

The community is also a repository of knowledge and skills which have evolved traditionally and these need to be integrated in the risk reduction process. It is necessary to educate the community about the entire disaster risk reduction and even to impart skills and assign specific roles to the members of the community, so that the first response from the community is a well coordinated one.

➤ 12.8.5 Focus on District Disaster Management Plan

The District Administration should discuss the hazard, risk and vulnerability profile of the district. The Administration should know the vulnerability map of the district, historical profile of various disasters that have happened in the past, their impact on the district and how the district was able to cope up. What is the preparedness of the district now? Would the district be able to handle the disaster if it is hit now? What is the present capacity of preparedness of the district administration or DDMA for search and rescue, relief distribution, logistics, ensuring life-line services, providing security and safety to the people, law and order situation, resource mobilisation, etc.? The administration needs to know the answers for all these questions. This would give an idea of the capacity of the district and also give direction to start planning. The administration or DDMA then consolidates the risks of the district and take the level forward.

12.9 Key Issues

12.9.1 The Uttarakhand Tragedy and the Lessons Learnt

Heavy rainfall over three days, 16-18 June 2013, along with a few cloudbursts caused the melting of Chorabari Glacier at the height of 3,800 metres and eruption of the river Mandakini which led to heavy floods and massive landslides along with heavy boulders near Kedarnath and few other areas of Uttarakhand, including Badrinath and Uttarkashi. It was the worst natural disaster in our country since the 2004 tsunami. The devastation in its wake has been huge but the largest impact has been at the temple town of Kedarnath. It is the downstream region along the Mandakini river. In the midst of the annual pilgrimage season, tens of thousands of people were present at the time of the incident. As a result, nearly four to six thousand people were feared killed and about a hundred thousand pilgrims and tourists were trapped in the valley for days because of damaged and blocked roads. The death toll, however, as per official records, is said to be nearly four thousand only. Entire villages and settlements, such as Gaurikund and the market town of Ram Bada, a transition point to Kedarnath, have been obliterated, while the market town of Sonprayag suffered heavy damage and loss of lives.

The Army, Air Force, Indo-Tibetan Border Police (ITBP), Border Security Force, National Disaster Response Force (NDRF), Public Works Department and local administration worked together for quick rescue operations. Several thousand soldiers were deployed for the rescue missions. Helicopters were used to rescue people, but due to rough terrain, heavy fog and rainfall, manoeuvring them was a challenge. The armed forces and paramilitary troops evacuated nearly one lakh people from the flood ravaged area. Operation Rahat was the name given to the Air Force's rescue operations. Operation Suryahope was the name given to the Army's rescue operations.

Unprecedented destruction by the rainfall witnessed in Uttarakhand was attributed to unscientific developmental activities undertaken in recent decades, contributing to high level of loss of property and lives. Roads constructed in haphazard style, new resorts and hotels built on fragile river banks and more than 70 hydro-electric projects in the watersheds of the state led to a 'disaster waiting to happen' situation. The tunnels built and blasts undertaken for the 70 hydro-electric projects contributed to the ecological imbalance in the state, with flows of river water restricted and the streamside development activity contributing to a higher number of landslides and more flooding. Existing infrastructure has been totally demolished. It has left border villages disconnected which certainly adds to our strategic concerns.

According to a 'Performance Audit of Disaster Preparedness in India', published by the Comptroller and Auditor General of India (CAG: Report No 5 of 2013), the following shortcomings of Uttarakhand were not only published but were taken up with the State Government as well, as a follow up. The main shortcomings pin-pointed by the CAG were:

1. In the state, the frequency and intensity of various disasters had not been identified.

2. State Disaster Management Authority (SDMA), headed by the Chief Minister, although constituted in October 2007, had not formulated any rules, regulations, policies and guidelines. State Executive Committee (SEC) was formed in January 2008 but 'never met since its creation' (this highlights the laxity and indifference). District Disaster Management Authority (DDMA) was constituted in Nainital in December 2007. Since inception, DDMA met only twice (April and May 2011). Thus, the state authorities were virtually non-functional.
3. The State Disaster Management Plan was under preparation and actionable programmes were not prepared for various disasters.
4. We noticed irregularities in the management of State Disaster Response Fund. These included non-investment of funds which resulted in potential loss of interest of Rs 9.96 crore during 2007-2012. There were delays ranging from 80 days to 184 days in the release of the Centre's share of funds during 2007-11 and no funds were released in 2011-12 as the state government did not submit utilisation certificates and annual report of natural calamity.
5. No plan was prepared in the state for early warning. The communication system was inadequate. This resulted in delayed information to vulnerable population.
6. Hazard Safety Cell of the state government had so far identified 7374 buildings in three cities out of which 1,109 buildings were found to be vulnerable to moderate earthquake. These buildings needed to be retrofitted, but no such measures were taken.
7. Geological Survey of India in June 2008 identified only 101 villages as vulnerable out of 233 disaster affected villages. No measures were taken by the State Government for their rehabilitation, despite a lapse of four years after their identification.
8. The State Government did not sanction any post for the State Disaster Management Authority which affected the establishment of the Management Information System. In the District Emergency Operation Centre (DEOC) at the district level, there was an acute shortage of manpower. In 13 districts, only 66 posts (56%) were filled against sanctioned manpower of 117 (9 posts each in 13 districts), and
9. It was also noticed that no master trainers were trained to impart training to the staff at the district, block and village levels engaged in the prevention and mitigation of disaster management. Medical personnel were also not trained in hospital preparedness for emergencies or mass casualty incident management.

The serious lapses that have been reported are a sad reflection of the state of affairs. It also shows that a lot of commitment, dedication and foresight is required in a state like Uttarakhand which is prone to almost all kinds of disasters except the threats from coastal areas and high seas.

Even more striking has been the realisation about how precious little has gone in the name of creating awareness and preparing all sections of the society for an eventuality like the June 2013 Uttarakhand disaster.

Besides preparedness, the response during crisis was also too slow. The Uttarakhand Government could not gauge the scale of tragedy in the initial two days. The state government did not have adequate evacuation capabilities. The evacuation work was mainly carried out by the Army, Air Force, Indo-Tibetan Border Police (ITBP), Border Security Force and National Disaster Response Force (NDRF). Search and rescue work also started very late.

Rehabilitation and reconstruction process was also very slow. It was mainly due to two reasons (a) roads and electricity lines were badly damaged so connectivity, communication and electricity services were totally disrupted, and (b) rain did not stop for a few days and so medical aid and food items were not supplied adequately as government machinery was waiting for the rain to stop. Even after October, rehabilitation work was not as per the desired pace.

Role of BSF in Rehabilitation Work

The BSF had adopted 12 villages for rehabilitation work. BSF made temporary bridges like foot bridges, rope bridges, Jhoola Pul (suspension bridge) on mountaineering patterns for connectivity. It helped in medical aid supply and ration supply for community kitchen. BSF jawans conducted rehabilitation work despite rains and heavy odds.

➤ 12.9.2 Was the Uttarakhand Tragedy Natural or Man-made?

Undoubtedly, it was a natural disaster which caught the administration and the local people by surprise. But many man-made mistakes compounded the problem. The major ones are given below:

1. **No control over the number of tourists and pilgrims reaching Kedarnath.** At the time of the tragedy it is believed that there were almost 5-10 times more people than the capacity of roads and towns.
2. **Unlimited construction on fragile river beds.** River beds are meant for rivers but due to unregulated developmental activities, haphazard constructions took place near river beds to cater to increasing number of tourists. This went on without any proper planning and norms of construction.
3. **Ecological imbalance.** The entire ecology of the region could have been disturbed due to rampant construction of roads, tunnels, dams and use of blast technology for construction.

Perhaps if we had been careful about the above factors, the scale of the tragedy could have been minimised.

➤ 12.9.3 Social and Emotional Problems Associated with Disasters

While dealing with disasters, we need to be particularly responsive to the emotional and social problems that people experience due to a disaster. Almost 10 per cent of the people affected by the tsunami – potentially half a million people – had mental health problems so severe that they required professional treatment. Psychosocial care deals with a broad range of emotional and social problems and helps in restoring social cohesion as well as independence and dignity of individuals and groups. It prevents pathologic developments and further social dislocations. Normalisation of emotional reaction is an important task in psychosocial care for the survivors of disasters. Emotional reactions such as guilt, fear, shock, grief, vigilance, numbness, intrusive memories, and despair are responses of people experiencing unforeseen disasters beyond their coping capacity. Emotional reactions are normal responses to an abnormal situation. Nearly 90 percent of survivors of a disaster experience these emotional reactions immediately after the disaster. Psychosocial care is essential for all these people.

PROBABLE QUESTIONS BASED ON THIS CHAPTER

1. What are the main phases of disaster management?
2. How can disaster risk be reduced in advance?
3. Write a short note on National Disaster Management Act (NDM Act) 2005.
4. What is the role of National Disaster Management Authority in disaster management?
5. How can district administration play a significant role in disaster management?